ADVANCE PRAISE FOR *BEE A GOOD HUMAN*

"Each page gives you a wry smile, a shot of joy,
and an appreciation for the little ones flying
and crawling around us. Ali's humor and wit pair
perfectly with a cup of coffee in the morning."
—Phil Torres, biologist, TV host

"An adorable new perspective on death."
—Phoebe Bridgers, musician

"A project filled with death and heartwarming inspiration."
—Josh Zoerner, the boy Ali was trying to impress

"Ali comes up with the kind of jokes that make
you say, 'I wish I had thought of that!'"
—Adam the Bee Guy

"There's an intimacy to Ali's work—and I'm not just talking
about when she posts pics of her bug-censored breasts on
Instagram. No, there's a sense of serenity and transparency to
pen on paper that adds texture and depth to Ali's relatable
quips and bits of wisdom. The dead bugs, juxtaposed
with pen strokes, are a simple and quirky reminder of our
perplexing place in this complex and fleeting universe."
—Peter Oren, musician

"I can bee whoever I want 2."
—Taylor Bennett, rapper

"A collection of death to bring warmth to your life."
—Jodie Langford, artist, Bode Burnout

"Dead bugs are the new life coaches."
—Mat Alano-Martin, comedian

"To discover someone's breath of creativity is usually unexpected. It takes time. Over the past two years, I've discovered Ali has a big, very big imagination. She creates social awareness through drawing, writing, and shaping important daily sayings. As a lover of insects, flies, butterflies, and bees, she creates mini dramas daily that are always personal and uplifting. I look forward to each day (yes, Ali posts a creative poetic image every day and sometimes more) to see her fascinating, uplifting, and private view of life. Art is always private, then becomes public. Thank you, Ali."
—Barry Gealt, artist

"Do you like books, funny jokes, and insects? Well, bee prepared to be amothed . . . amazed! The art is creative, the jokes are timeless, and the insects are dead (they were found that way). There is a *Mean Girls* reference in this book that especially tickled my funny bone. This book belongs on your shelf, table, or in your hands this minute!"
—Spark Tabor, comedian

"I spend all my time around comedians, so in looking for 'other' types of Instagram accounts, I came across Ali's SoFlyTaxidermy. At first, I didn't even know she was in Bloomington! With over 100k followers, I just assumed she was from somewhere else. What's interesting is in looking to get away from comedians in my social media scrolling, Ali has made me laugh as much as any comedian."
—Jared Thompson, owner,
The Comedy Attic, Bloomington, IN

"Ali's work reminds us that mortality is absolutely inevitable, but perhaps if we're lucky, someone might come along and use our rigid dead bodies to spread joy."
—Tyler Thrasher, professional mad scientist

"A beautiful look inside the modern mind of entomology."
—Kendall Long, reality star contestant,
The Bachelor and *Bachelor in Paradise*

"You've probably never considered how much you have in common with an insect—that bees like the flowers on your windowsill as much (or more!) than you or that butterflies aren't the only ones who go through metamorphosis (hello middle school awkward phase). Ali Beckman created a guidebook for better living starring these insects to show us that the little pollinators are more powerful than you think. Beckman's delightfully humorous and thoughtful work will remind you to treat yourself and all Earth's creatures with kindness, and as all flies would agree, sometimes 'going through shit' isn't all that bad."
—Lily & Madeleine, musicians

"Ali's artwork is beautifully minimal and witty with a refreshing feminist twist. It's the perfect addition to any coffee table. Bee-ware, this book may inspire you to start collecting dead bugs . . ."
—The Orbit Room, Bloomington, IN

"Ali Beckman is a true artist, a lover of nature, a keen eye, and a creative genius. Ali's book, *Bee a Good Human*, has completely won my heart; her incredible ability to compose the deceased insects of the world into the most glorious, uplifting, and hilarious conversations makes this book truly unique. Long live the Earth's most underrated creatures, and may Ali bring them to life in the most remarkable ways for volumes to come. *Bee a Good Human* is the perfect book for anyone who has ever wondered about the secret life of animals and found joy in imagining their existence to be equally as fraught, complicated, and wondrous as our own."
—Ben Moore, Ben's Bees

 a
good
hvman

 a
good
human

A Pollinators' Guide to a Better Life

Ali Beckman

RED ⚡ LIGHTNING BOOKS

This book is a publication of

Red Lightning Books
1320 East 10th Street
Bloomington, Indiana 47405 USA

redlightningbooks.com

This book is printed on acid-free paper.

Manufactured in China

First printing 2021

ISBN 978-1-68435-132-9 (hardback)
ISBN 978-1-68435-133-6 (ebook)

No animals were harmed in the making of this book.

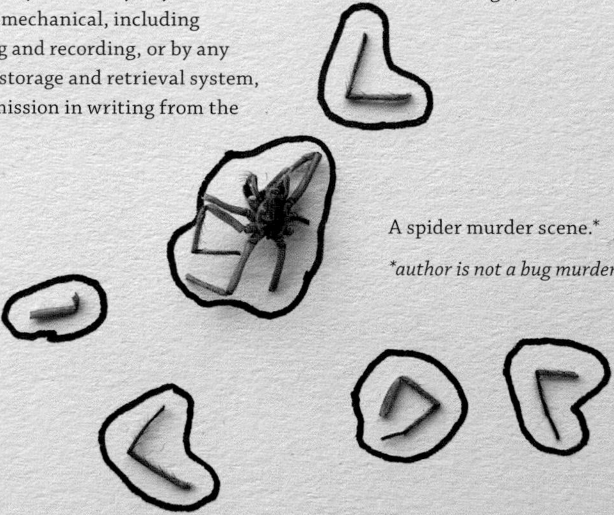

A spider murder scene.*

author is not a bug murderer

To Lillian, Landon, Claire, Caroline, and Blythe

FOREWORD

My name is Kate, and I keep dangerous insects in small boxes—in public. When they inevitably die (an individual honeybee's life span is quite short, about six weeks), I sometimes give them to my friend Ali.

Honeybees, and bees in general, often get a bad rap. I blame this almost entirely on the misrepresentation of bees in the 1991 American coming-of-age film *My Girl*, starring Macaulay Culkin. The entire movie rests on the premise that Culkin's character is deathly allergic to bees, and he dies a horrible death because he accidentally steps on a "bee's nest." Go back and watch the film; that's definitely a hornet's nest. This kind of anti-bee propaganda has been used for ages in films and television, damaging the bee's image.

Don't get me wrong, I am 100 percent pro-hornet. Hornets eat garden pests and are both valuable pollinators and living creatures. I actually have a soft spot for all misunderstood creatures: spiders, wolves, heck, I even like opossums. This urge to spin positive PR for the animal kingdom's most misrepresented creatures is what drove me to start my organization, Bee Public, back in 2013 with an emphasis on the importance of all nectar-sipping creatures (aka pollinators).

Bees and other pollinators are important to our ecosystem and to our everyday food supply. One in three bites of food we eat is made possible by a process called pollination. Basically, because plants can't walk across your yard to have sex, they rely on pollinators to get down and dirty on their behalf. When a pollinator—let's say a bee—visits a flower to sip the sweet nectar, pollen sticks to her fuzzy body and then is transferred to the next flower she visits. The pollen fertilizes that plant, making it possible to produce fruits, veggies, nuts, or seeds. She may perform the deed for up to five thousand flowers in one day! Voyeuristic as it may be, I enjoy watching this process firsthand on my urban farm.

Unfortunately, pollinators are having a tough go of it and have been for quite some time. They are disappearing all over the world due to pesticides, pollution, climate change, and lack of food. This poses a threat not only to our own food supply but also to our environment as a whole, as all flowering plants rely on pollinators to survive.

All types of bugs suffer when poisoned with pesticides, harmful chemicals designed to kill "bad" bugs. Pesticides weaken pollinators' immune systems, leaving them vulnerable to parasites and diseases. A changing climate can bring weather that's too wet or too dry and can affect the availability of flowers on which pollinators depend.

These are big problems that can be fixed with small solutions that anyone can take part in from their own backyard. Creating pollinator-friendly habitats, free from harmful chemicals such as pesticides and herbicides, provides pollinators with a healthy food source and a safe place to live.

Honeybees often get the spotlight when we talk about "saving the bees," but I think it's important to note that there are more than four thousand species of native bees in North America who need just as much, if not more, saving as our honey-making friends—not to mention butterflies, flies, bats, and hummingbirds. One of my favorite native bees is a hole-nesting bee called the mason bee. Mason bees know how to have a good time; they belly flop right into the middle of flowers, splashing pollen everywhere, making them one hundred times more effective at pollinating than honeybees.

One thing I do admire about honeybees is their altruism. At all costs, honeybees will work together to defend the colony, forage, and feed each other. When a honeybee stings, she dies. Only female honeybees have stingers (badass), which are actually her modified reproductive organs (double badass). The stinger is barbed and often gets caught on her target, damaging her internal organs and ultimately causing her own demise. Because it ends in a gruesome death, honeybees only use stinging as a last-ditch effort to protect their colony, but it's always for the greater good of the hive.

A honeybee colony is often referred to as a superorganism, an organized society that functions as an organic whole. Some beekeepers take this to mean that if an individual bee dies, it's more like when we lose a toenail. I don't buy it.

When I first started keeping honeybees seven years ago, I was warned about the dangers of anthropomorphization, or how humans portray the natural world as reflections of themselves. Some folks think it can lead to an inaccurate understanding of biological processes. As someone who grew up idolizing Dr. Doolittle, this advice was hard to swallow. And I get it, I really do. Assigning human qualities to animals is how people end up with twenty backyard tigers. But I refuse to let go of every morsel of the romance involved in forging a relationship with the animal world. (Note: This does not make *Bee Movie* okay. Don't even get me started on *Bee Movie*.)

Ali may have started off doing bug drawings as a way to impress a guy, but she ended up catching so much more in her web. Her knack for breathing humor and new life into small creatures that are often overlooked, both in life and in death, caught my eye, and we soon became virtual bug buddies.

Roger Ebert is known for saying, "Movies are the most powerful empathy machine in all the arts," because they can give you glimpses into other people's worlds. Whether your empathy machine is built from humor and deceased insects or something else entirely, I believe the world can never have enough. Empathy might be the only thing to motivate us as humans to act more like a honeybee and do what's right for the greater good.

KATE FRANZMAN
Bee Public
beepublic.com

ACKNOWLEDGMENTS

Thank you to my family. To my mom and dad for their love, support, and enthusiasm. Thank you to Courtney, Kylie, and Caleb.

Thank you to my friends. To Jackie Simmons and Anna Wolak for looking at my work with honesty. Thank you to Chance Lewandoski for all your encouragement. Thank you to my friends for their endless support, especially to Kathy Cook, Leigh Isaac, Natalie Webb, Jen Solomon, Alicia Jewell, Ashly O'Neil, Joanna Simms, Anna Stoddard, Jenna Hewitt, Erin Thomas, Eryn Blair, and Marian Hartmann.

Thank you to all my followers and to everyone who has sent me dead bugs.

Thank you to Rachel Rosolina for pushing this project. Thank you to everyone who has worked on this book. Thank you to everyone who has made this possible.

Thank you to Kate Franzman for sharing your knowledge on bees, not only with me but with everyone.

And lastly, thank you to Josh Zoerner. This idea would have never come about if I hadn't been trying to impress you.

 a good hvman

INTRODUCTION

So Fly Taxidermy started over four years ago in December of 2016. I came home one day and found two dead flies lying next to each other. I couldn't get over the image of the two flies having a conversation before they died. So, I grabbed a piece of paper, picked up the flies, got my pen out, and started drawing.

Since that day, I've studied entomology and the impact insects have in our world. The influence insects have on our ecosystem is truly remarkable. Through my pictures, I have been able to spread awareness and, in some cases, joy.

I use insects that have been found dead, given to me dead, or purchased dead. Although I have been accused of murdering insects for my project, I stand by ethically, morally, and sustainably resourcing them. I have been sent a scorpion from Arizona, flies from all over the United States, and moths from Washington and Kentucky. The audience I have built on Instagram is a community of bug lovers and an army of entomology enthusiasts who support my work and in turn find and send me insects.

My main goal with this project has always been to make people laugh. However, as it has grown and progressed, the awareness I have brought to the environment is an added bonus. People write to me daily with stories of how they have caught and released insects instead of just automatically killing them.

Typically, honeybees are thought of as the only pollinator worth saving, but pollinators come in all shapes and sizes! Pollinators are a huge part of So Fly Taxidermy, and I love that even flies pollinate. Did you know a tiny midge (a cousin to flies) pollinates chocolate? What a fun fact that we should all know! Flies sometimes get a bad rap, but I like to bring light to the situation by recognizing flies as a huge part of why our world goes round. Not only do flies pollinate but they also decompose tons and tons of agricultural waste that our world would not be able to handle on its own.

Insects and their contribution to our ecosystem are hard to ignore after you get down to the basics. Without humans, the planet would continue on; without insects, however, the environment is sure to collapse. With So Fly Taxidermy, through the puns and fun and laughter it brings, my main goal is to bring awareness to our little friends that make our world continually go round. With So Fly Taxidermy, I can show that spiders, beetles, roaches, ants, and even mosquitoes are essential!

This book is a lighthearted collection of So Fly Taxidermy and the powerful impact and joy insects bring to our planet. My hope is to make you think of the bigger picture and to laugh a little.

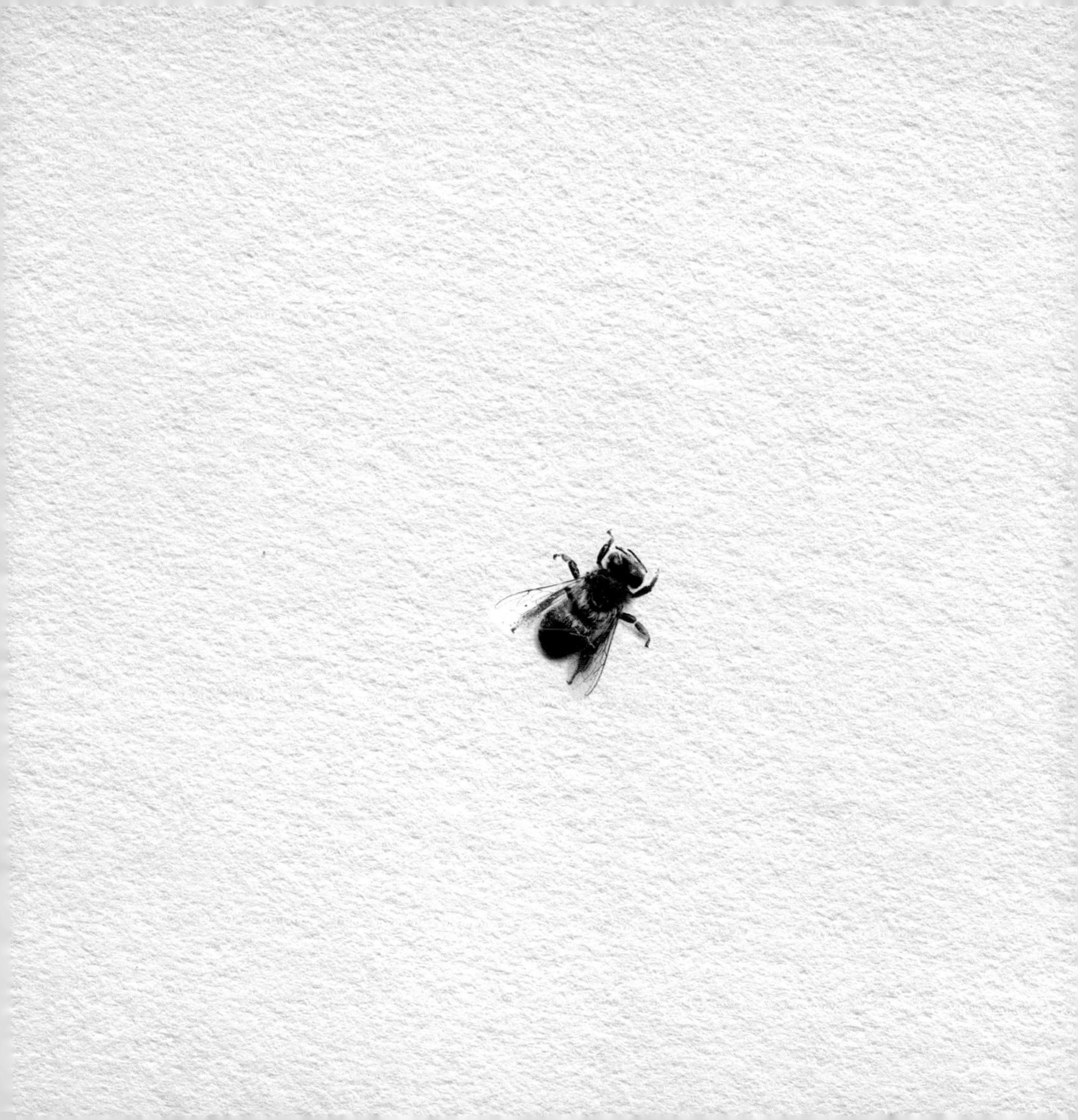

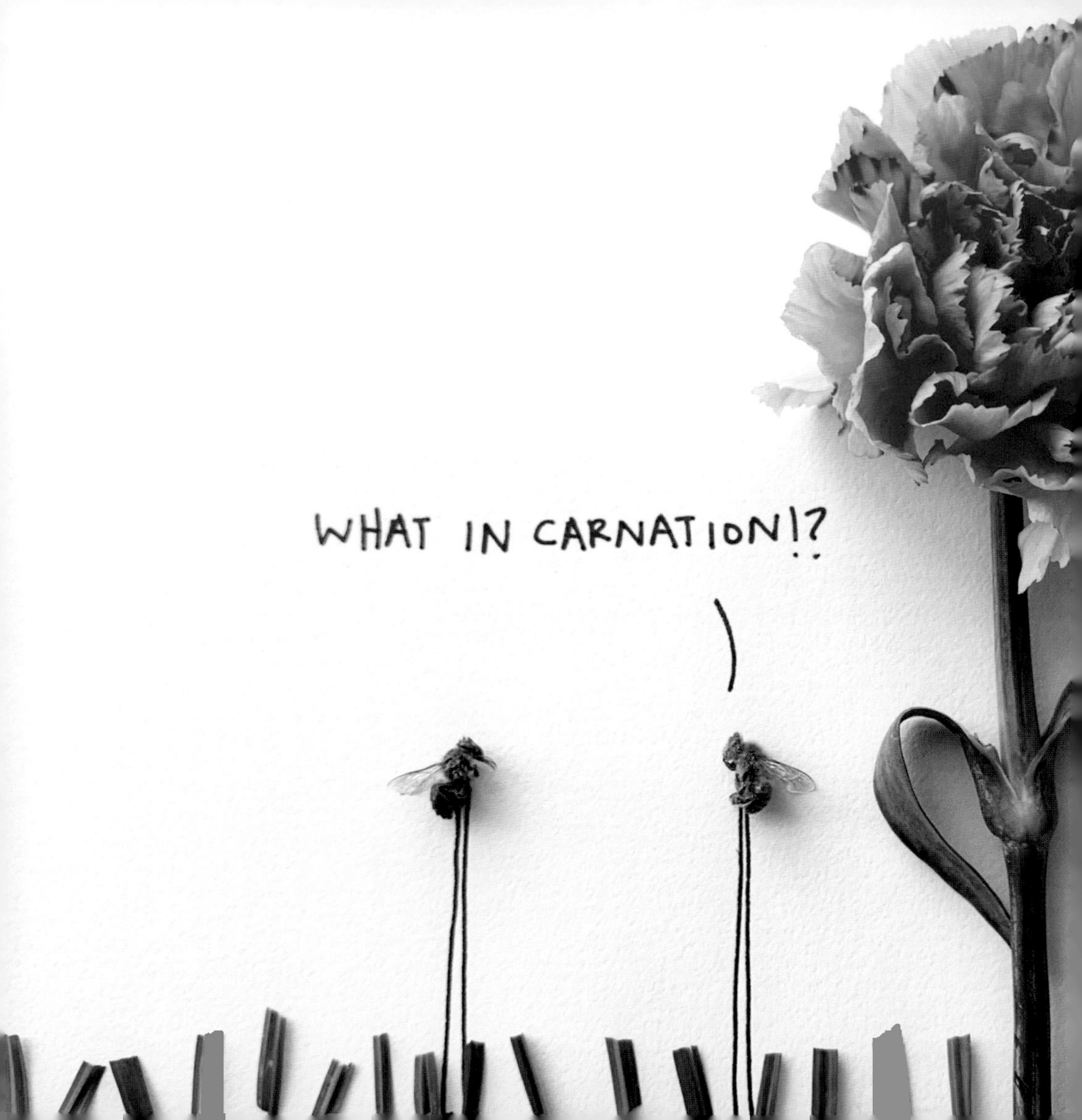
WHAT IN CARNATION!?

When you're shocked
but also a bee.

Behind the scenes.

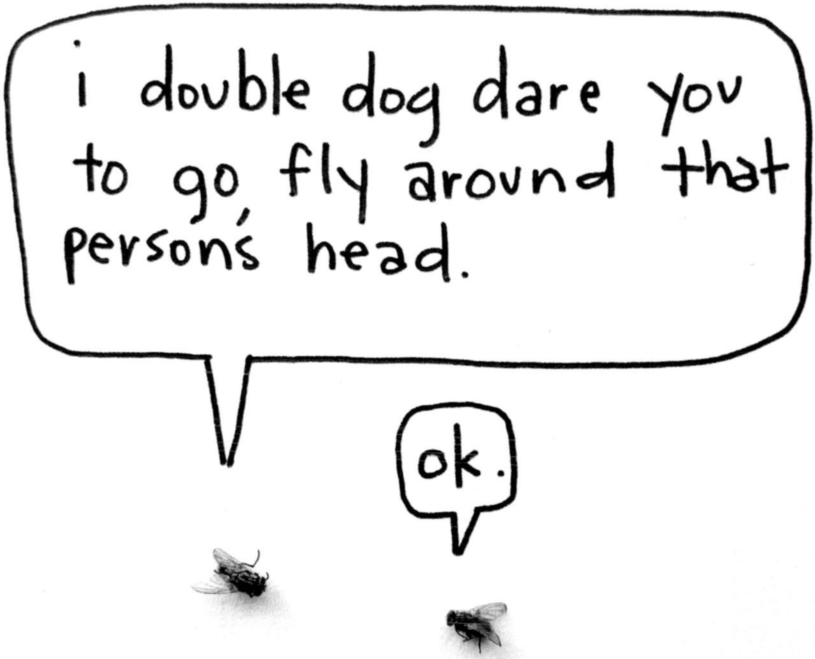
i double dog dare you to go, fly around that person's head.
ok.

CHANGE LOOKS DIFFERENT
ON EVERYONE.

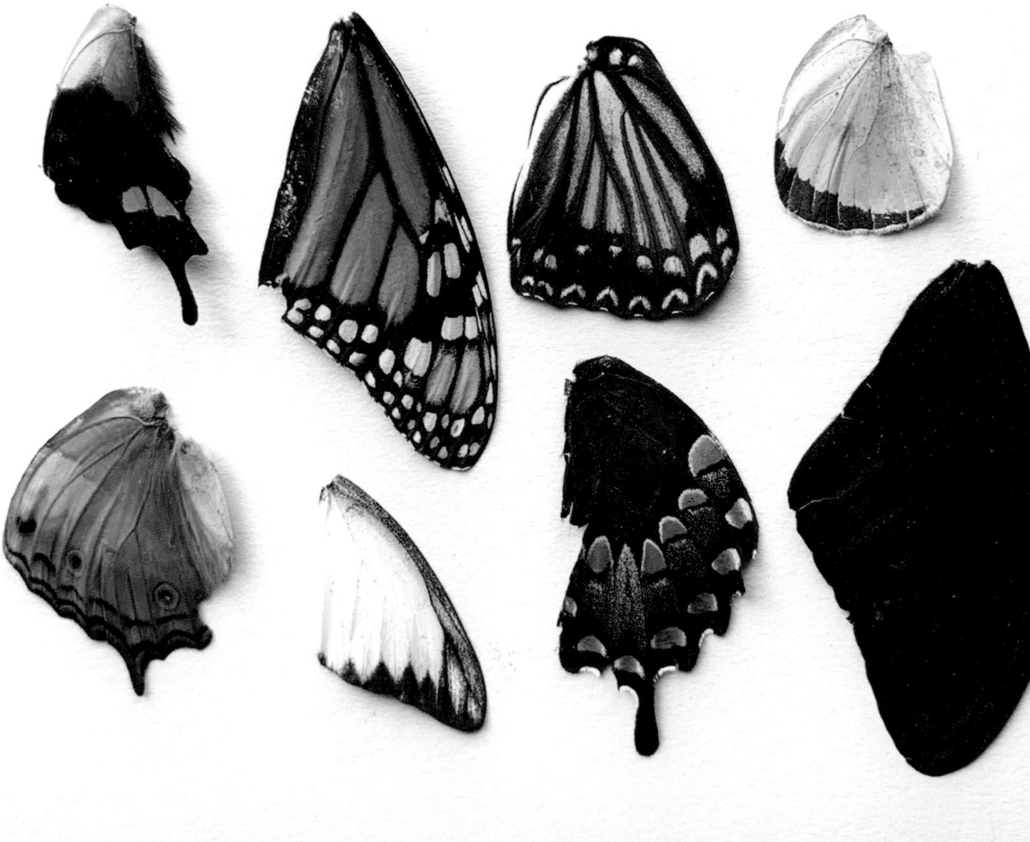

We're all different, and that's beautiful.

BEFORE COFFEE

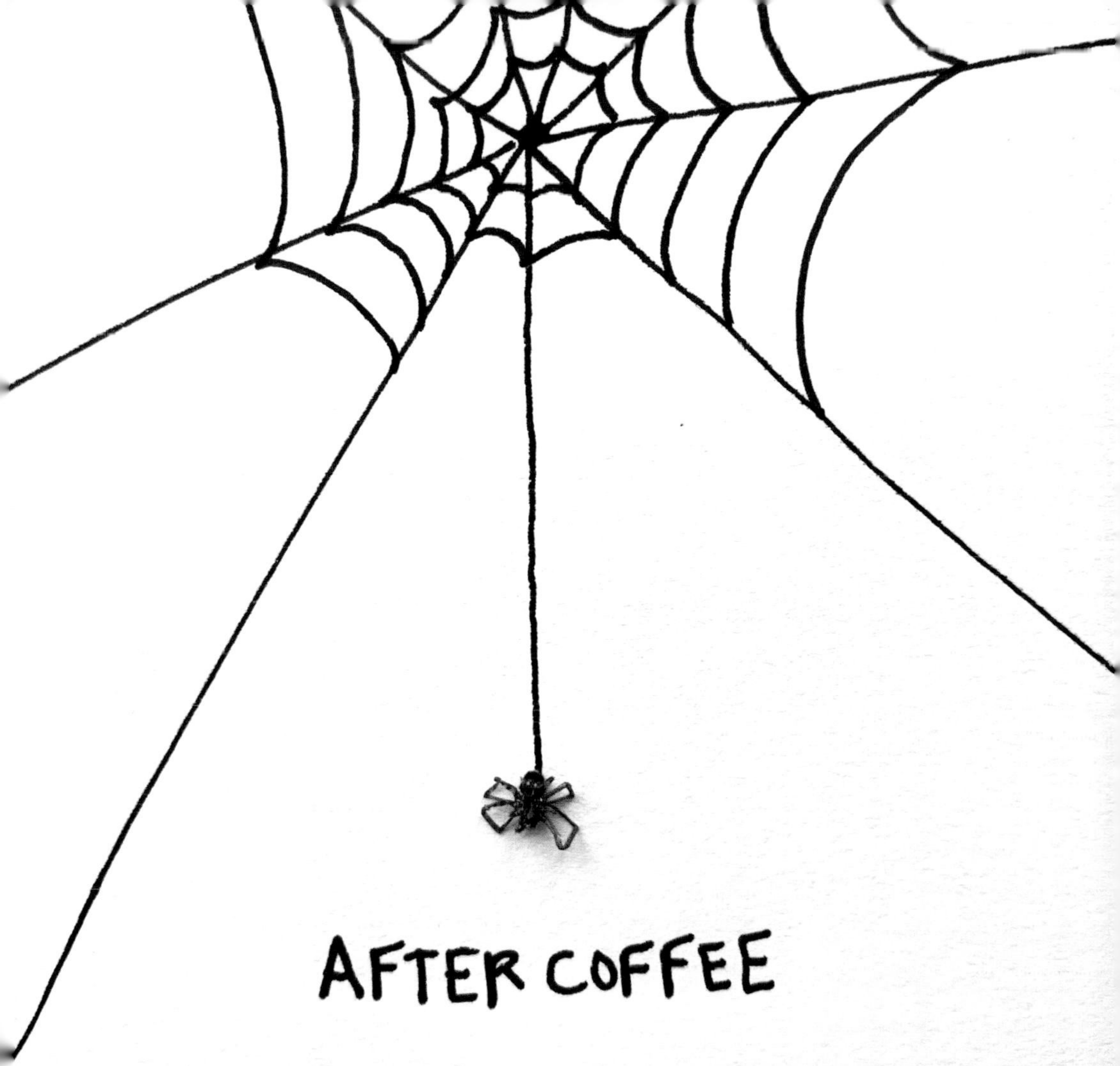
AFTER COFFEE

How to ask out a fruit fly with success.

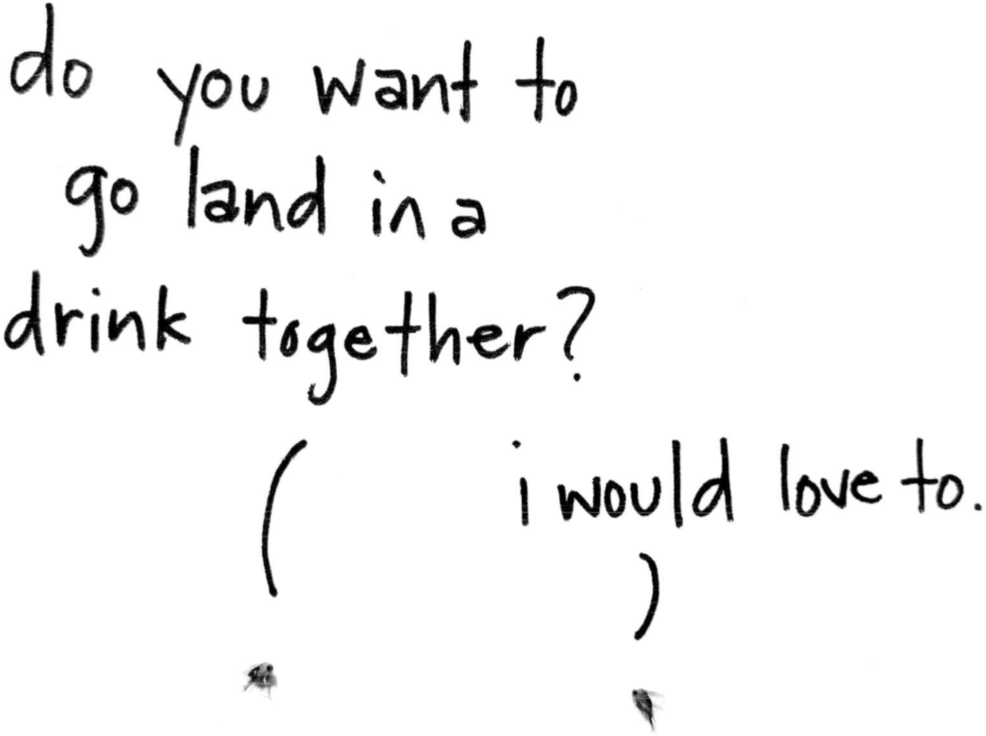
do you want to go land in a drink together?
i would love to.

moth,but make it fashion.

It's called moth fashion, sweetie. Look it up.

Bees can actually get drunk on pollen.
So drunk, in fact, "bouncer" bees will not
let them in the hive until they've sobered up!

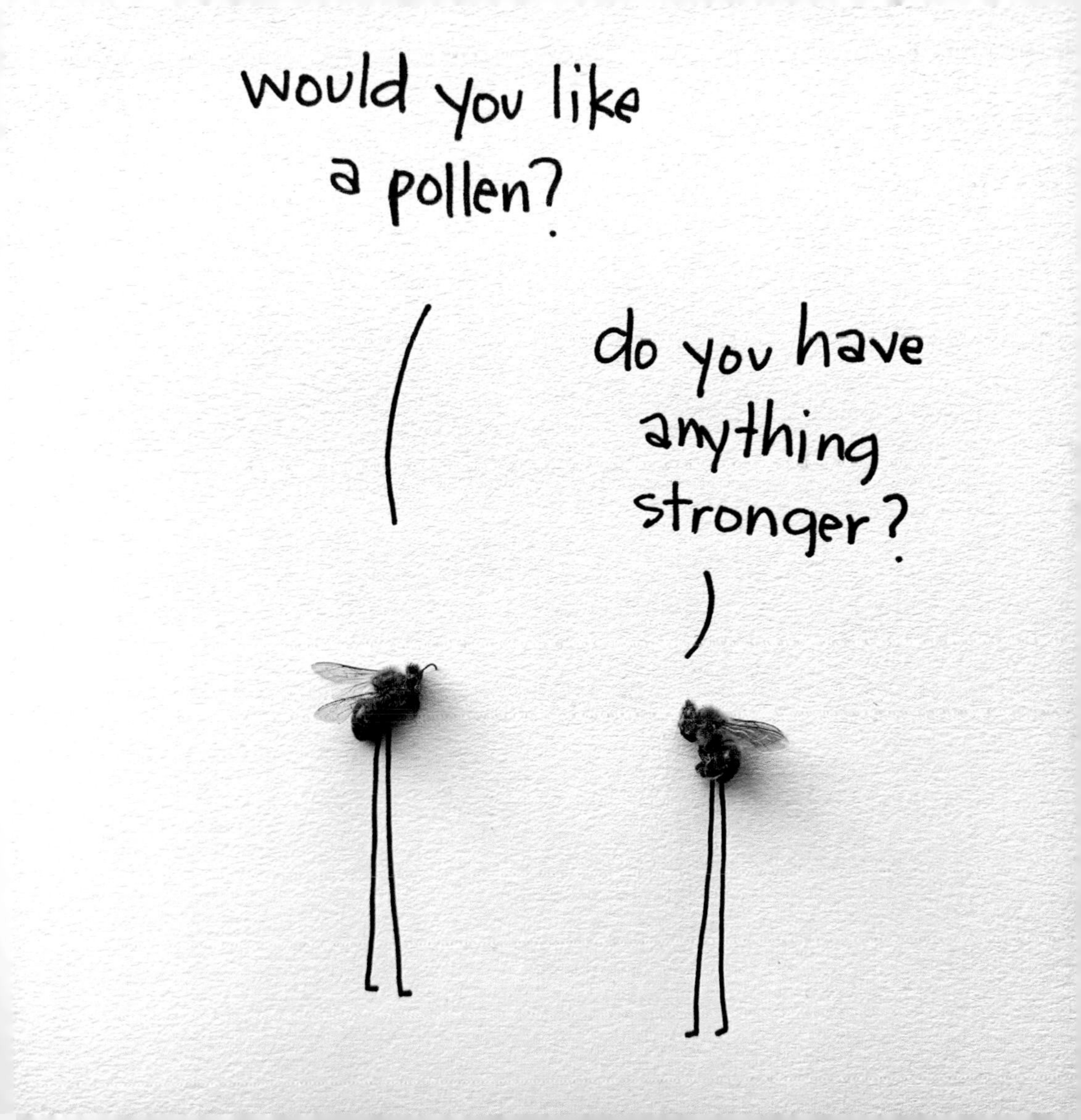
would you like a pollen?
do you have anything stronger?

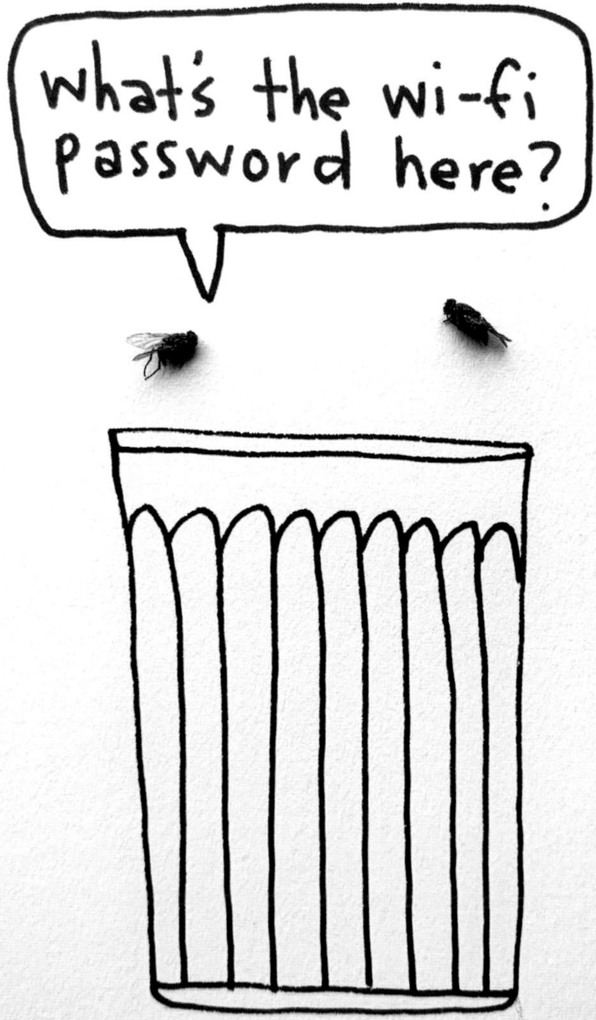
what's the wi-fi password here?

Seriously, I'm not going to use my data in this garbage can.

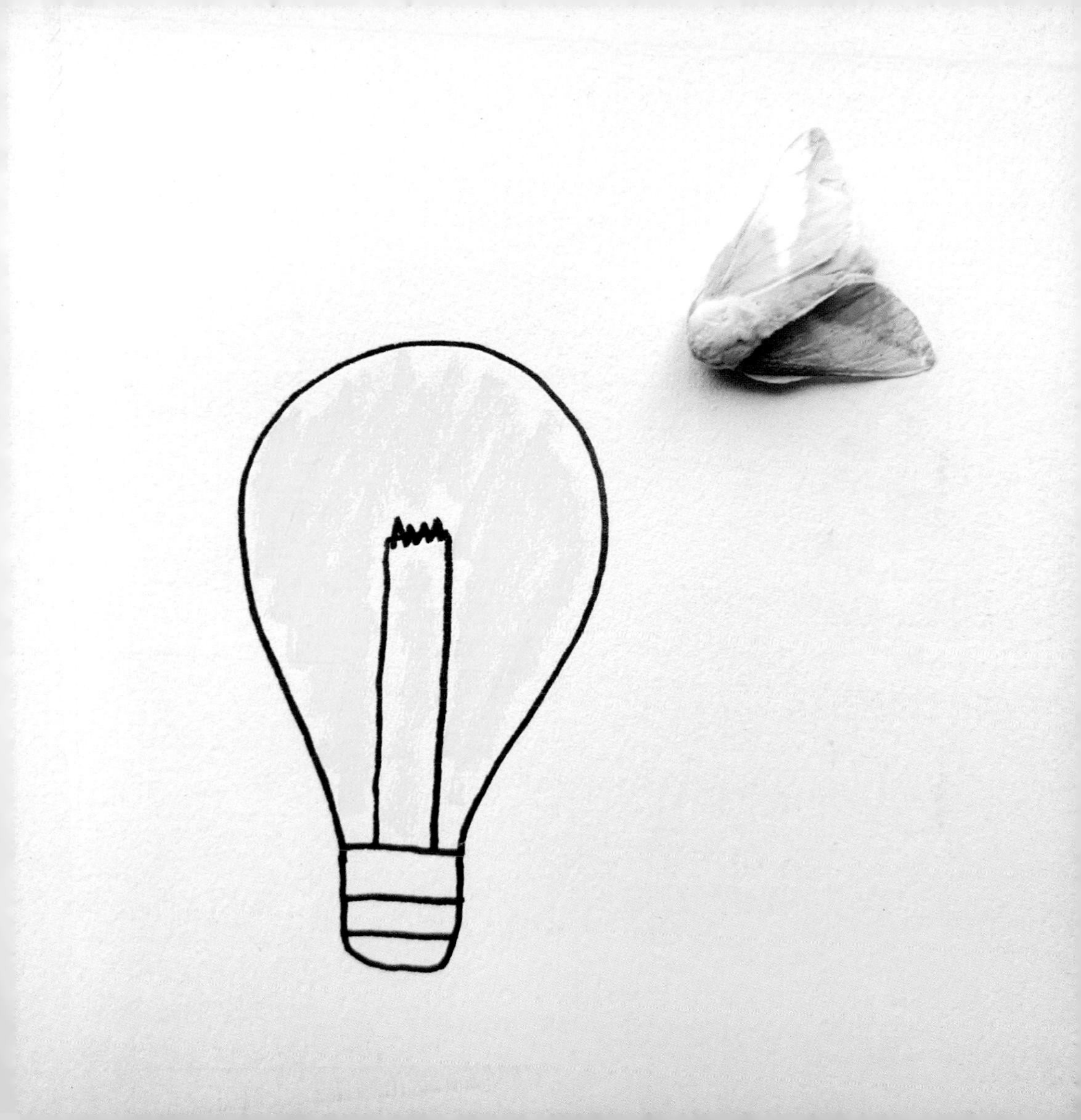

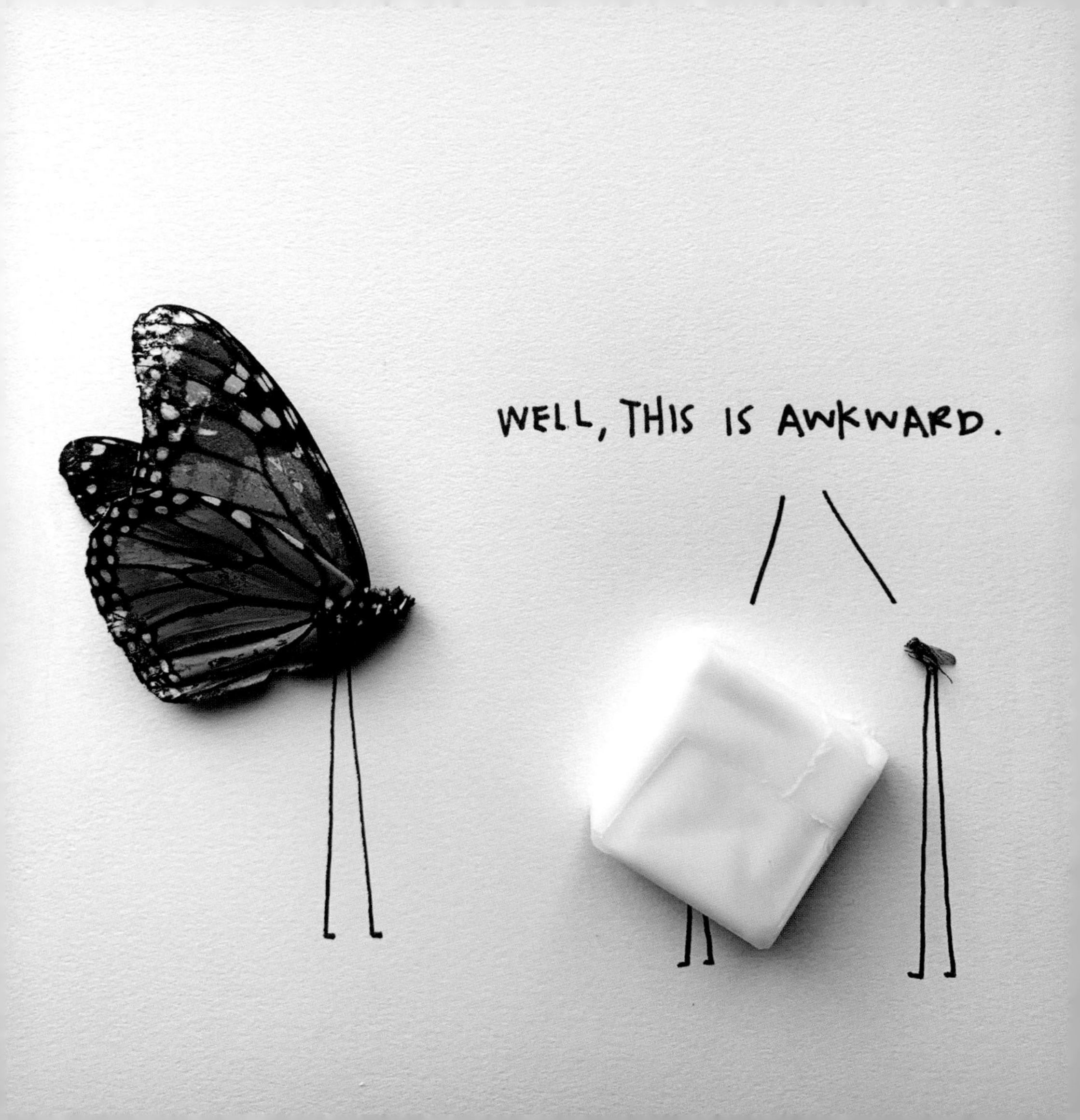
WELL, THIS IS AWKWARD.

Butterfly vs. butter fly.

Someone's gotta be.

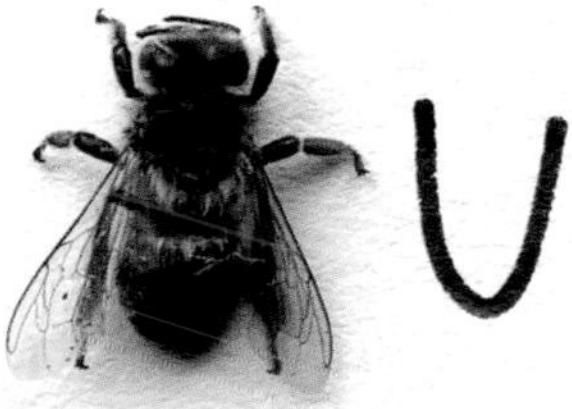
U

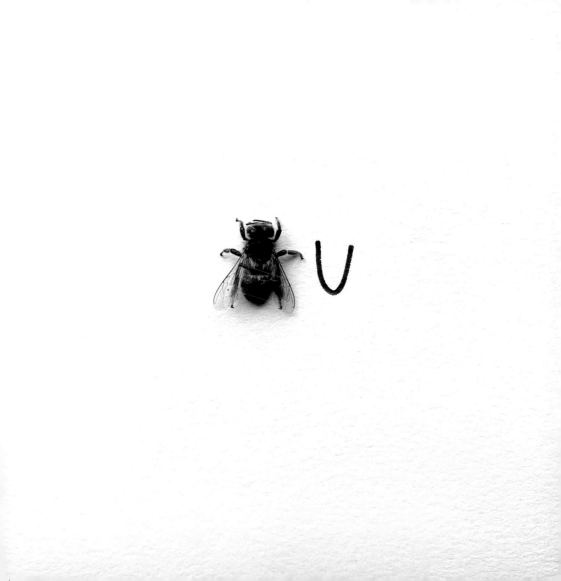

TEN QUINTILLION

10,000,000,000,000,000,000

USED IN A SENTENCE:
THERE ARE OVER TEN QUINTILLION
INSECTS IN THE WORLD.

STRAIGHT LINE

DOTTED LINE

- - - - - - - - -

SQUIGGLY LINE

BEE LINE

Love a good line.

Did you know flies are pollinators, too? Yeah, they eat decomposing matter, but they also serve a great purpose: pollinating!

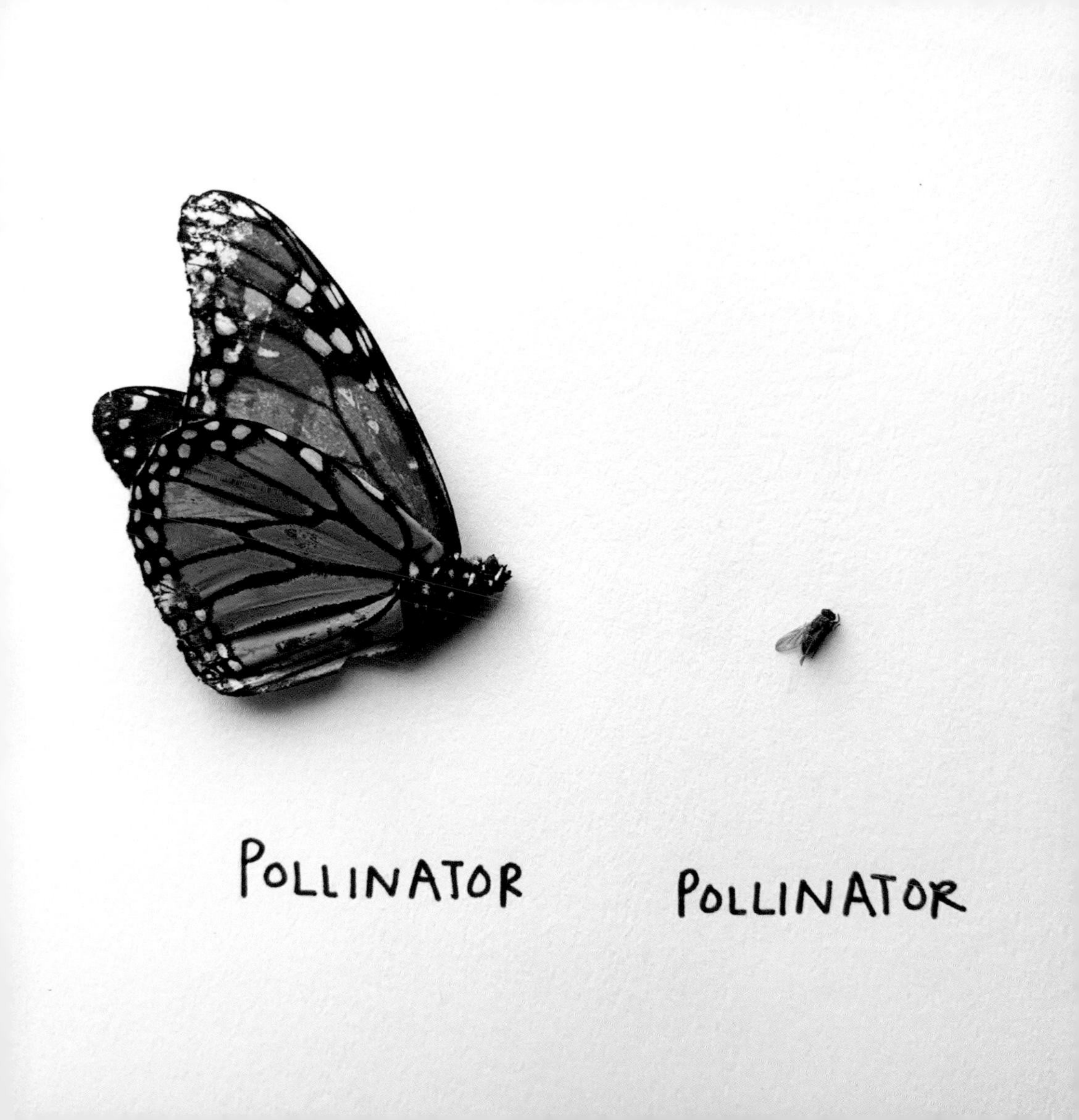
POLLINATOR
POLLINATOR

I NEED BUTTERFLIES
AND ALL YOU'RE
GIVING ME IS CRICKETS.

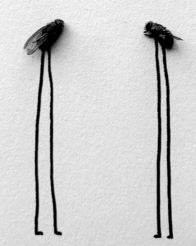

If you're giving me bugs,
they'd better be butterflies.

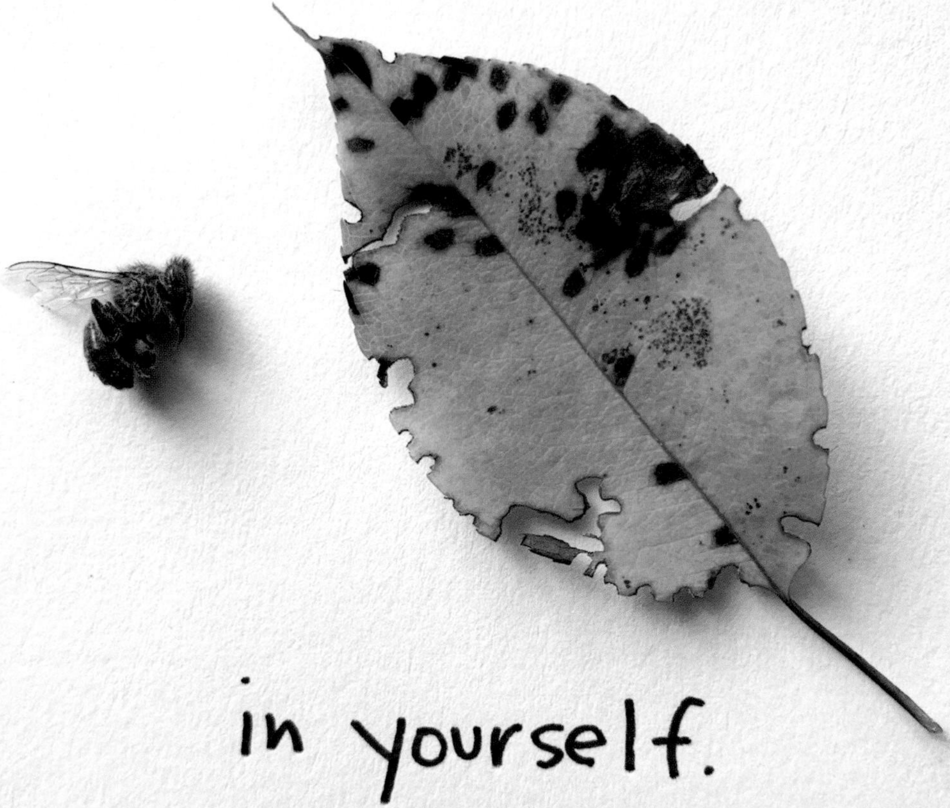

in yourself.

Bee leaf in yourself.

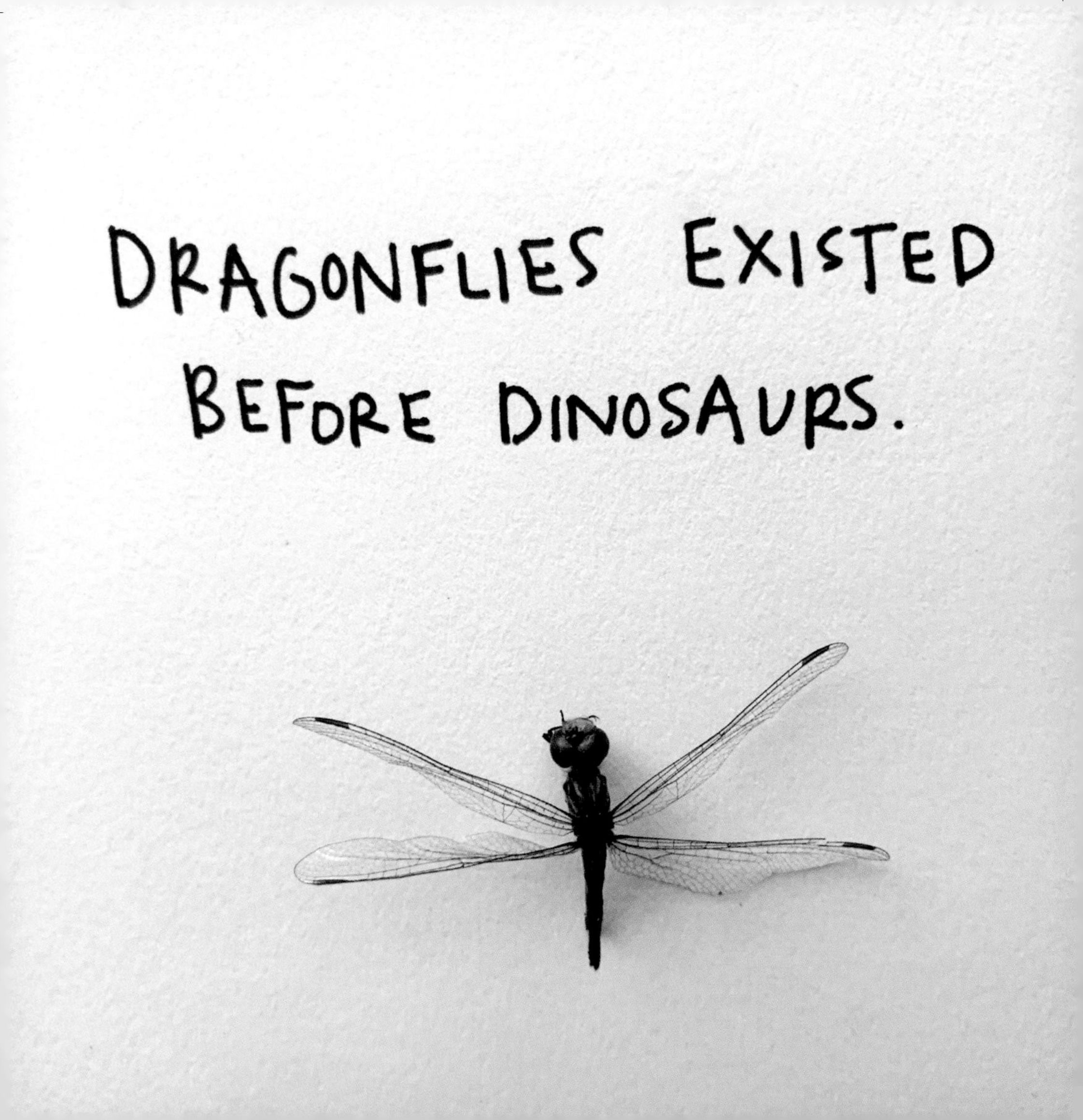
DRAGONFLIES EXISTED
BEFORE DINOSAURS.

I bet you were today years old
when you learned this.

The moment you ask a question
that's none of your business.

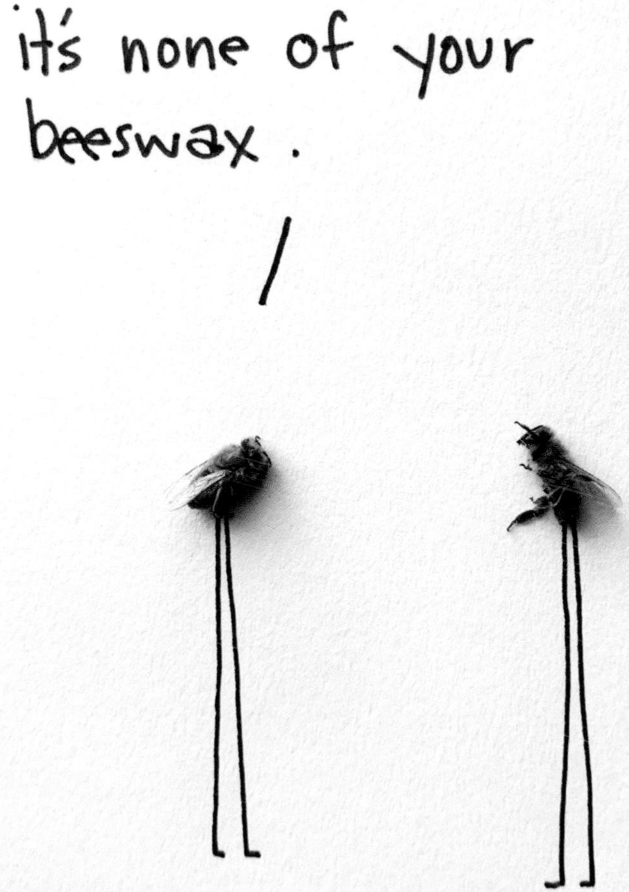
it's none of your
beeswax.

ON WEDNESDAYS
WE WEAR PINK.

You can't sit with us.

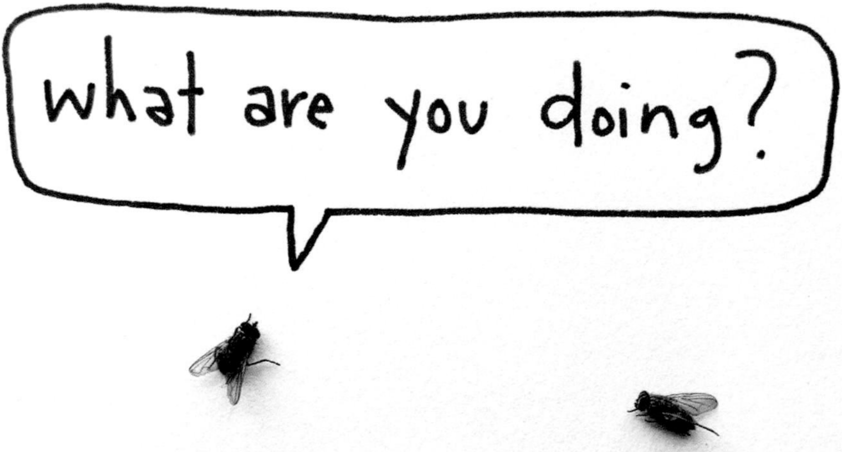
what are you doing?

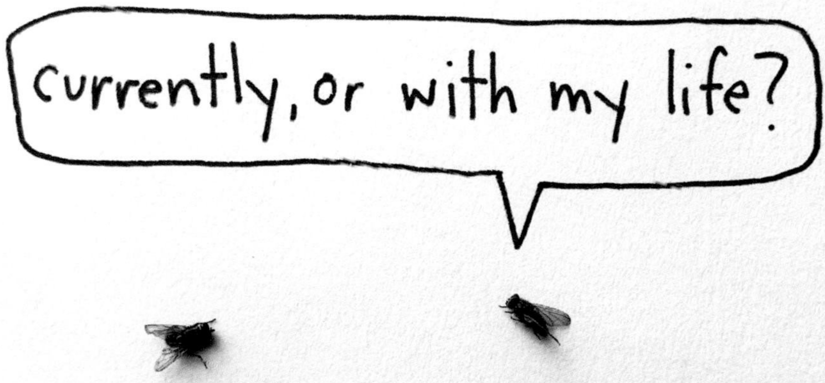
currently, or with my life?

Boob + bees = boobees

Arachnid relationship advice.

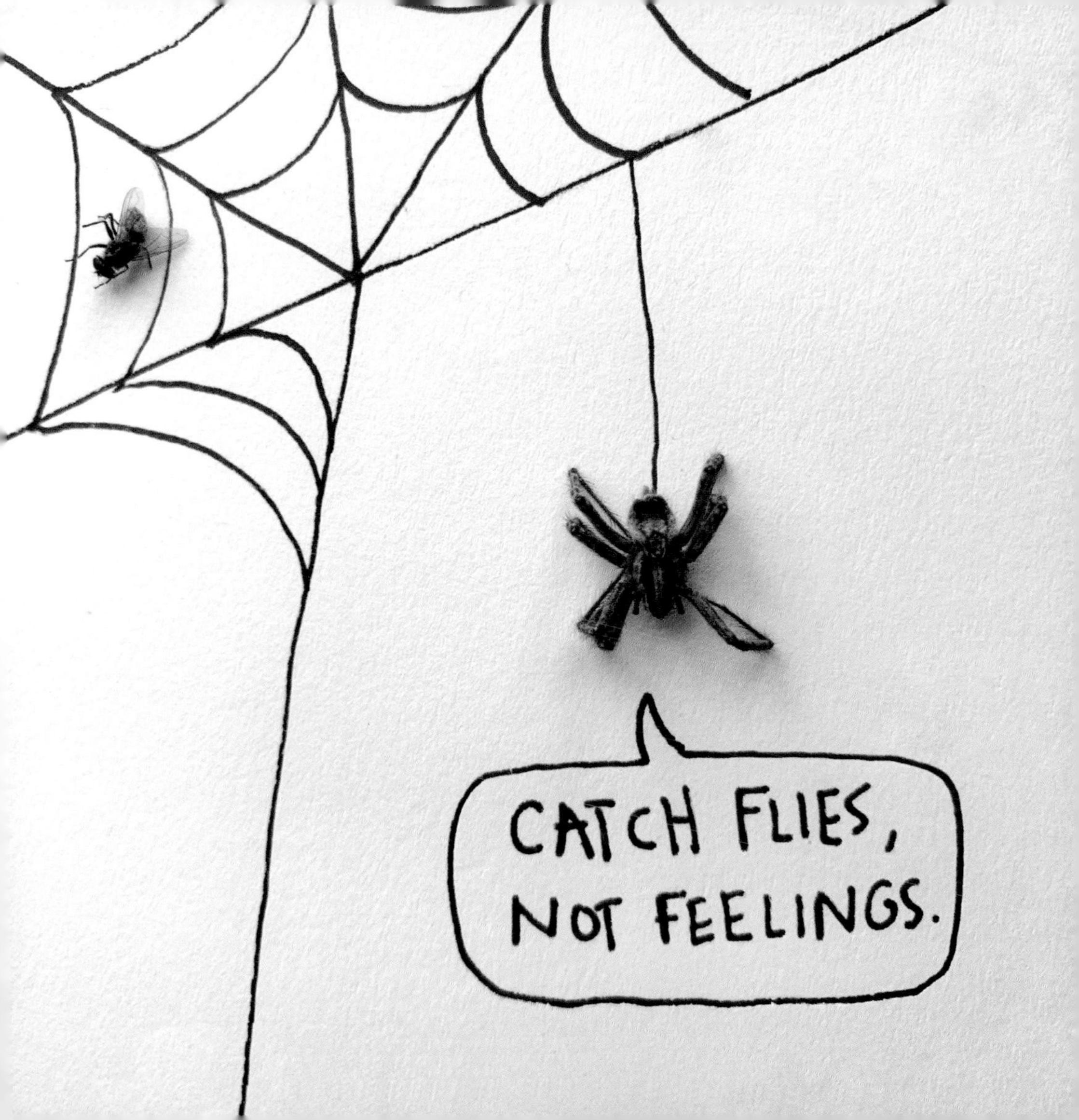
CATCH FLIES,
NOT FEELINGS.

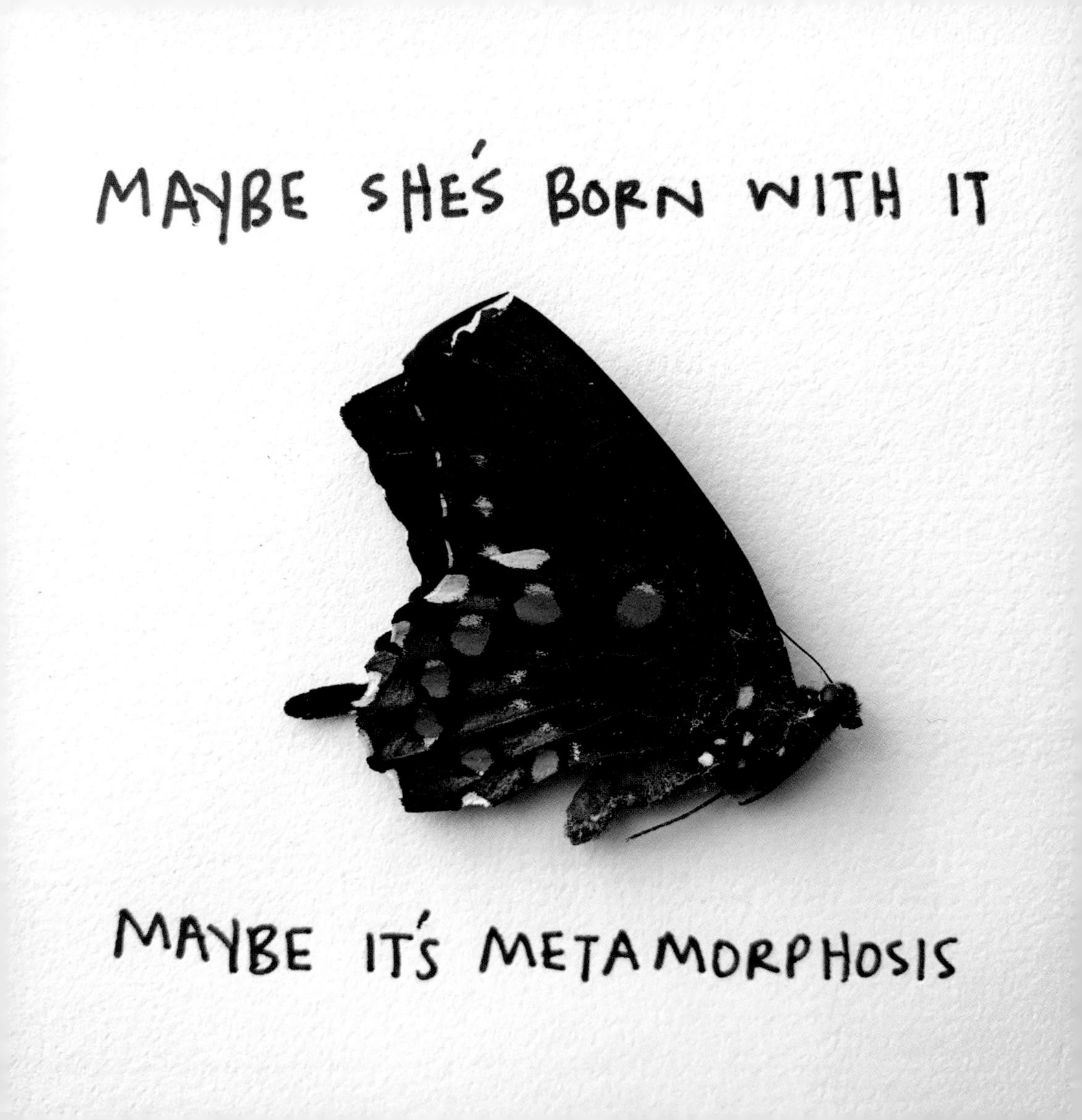
MAYBE SHE'S BORN WITH IT
MAYBE IT'S METAMORPHOSIS

Maybe it's both.

The female honeybee produces $\frac{1}{12}$ tablespoon of honey in her lifetime.

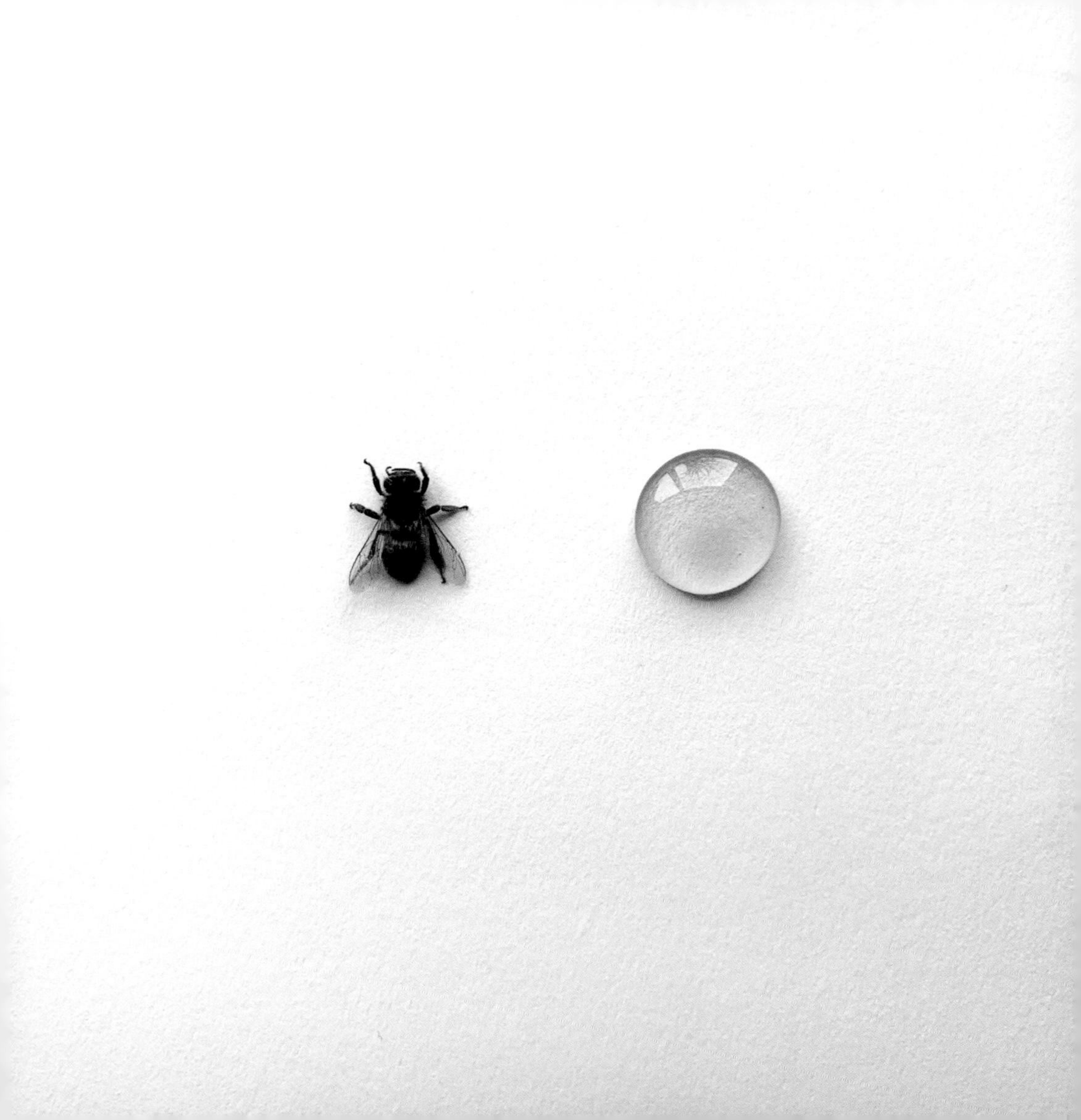

how to fly:

become reincarnated
as a fly.

Or get your pilot's license?
Either way works.

Here are nine cute snails for
your viewing pleasure.

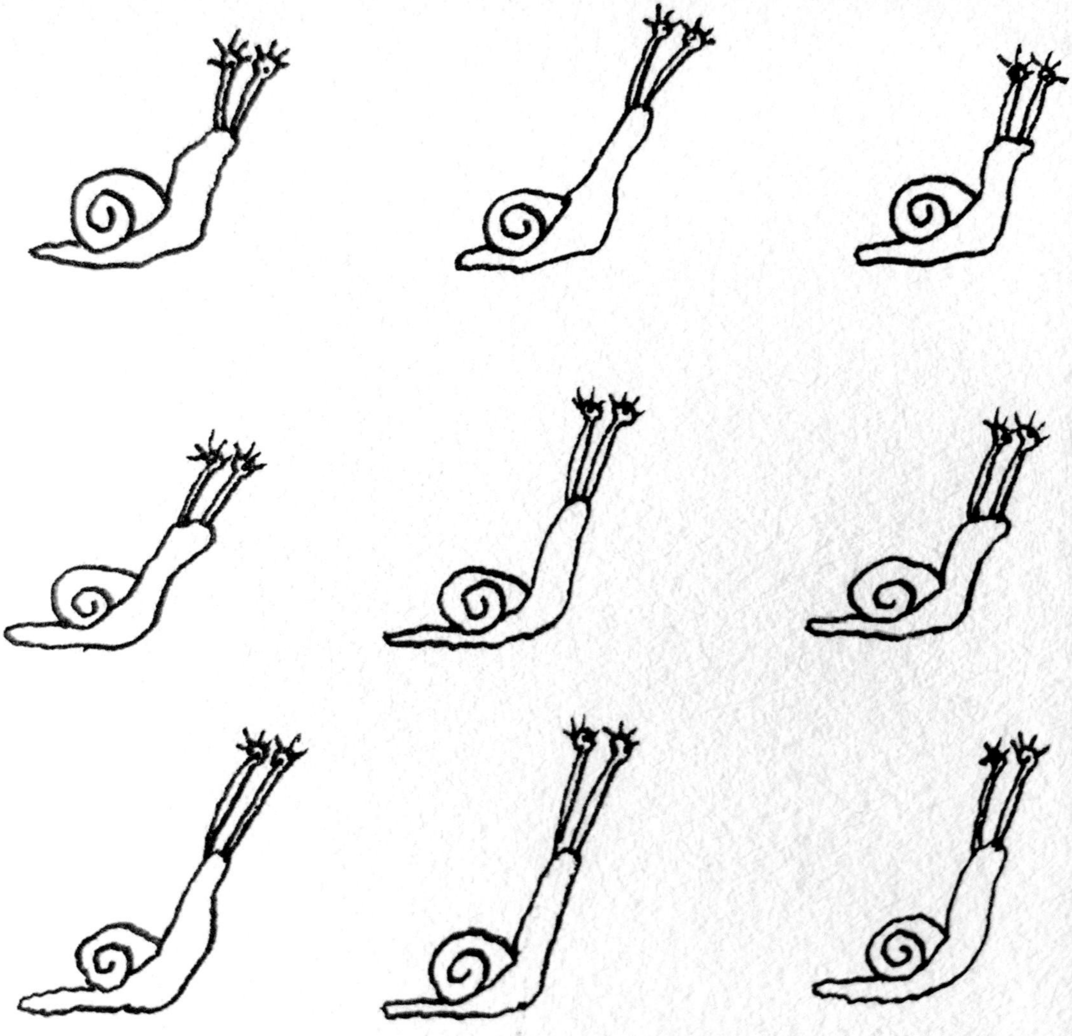

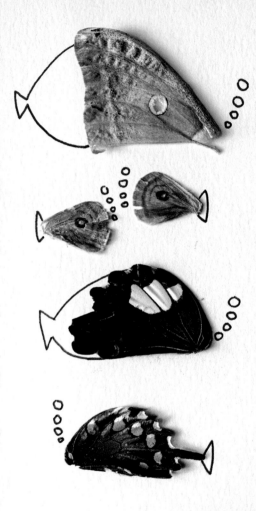

one fish,

two fish,

has a little bit of red
in it fish,

metallic blue fish.

Go fish.

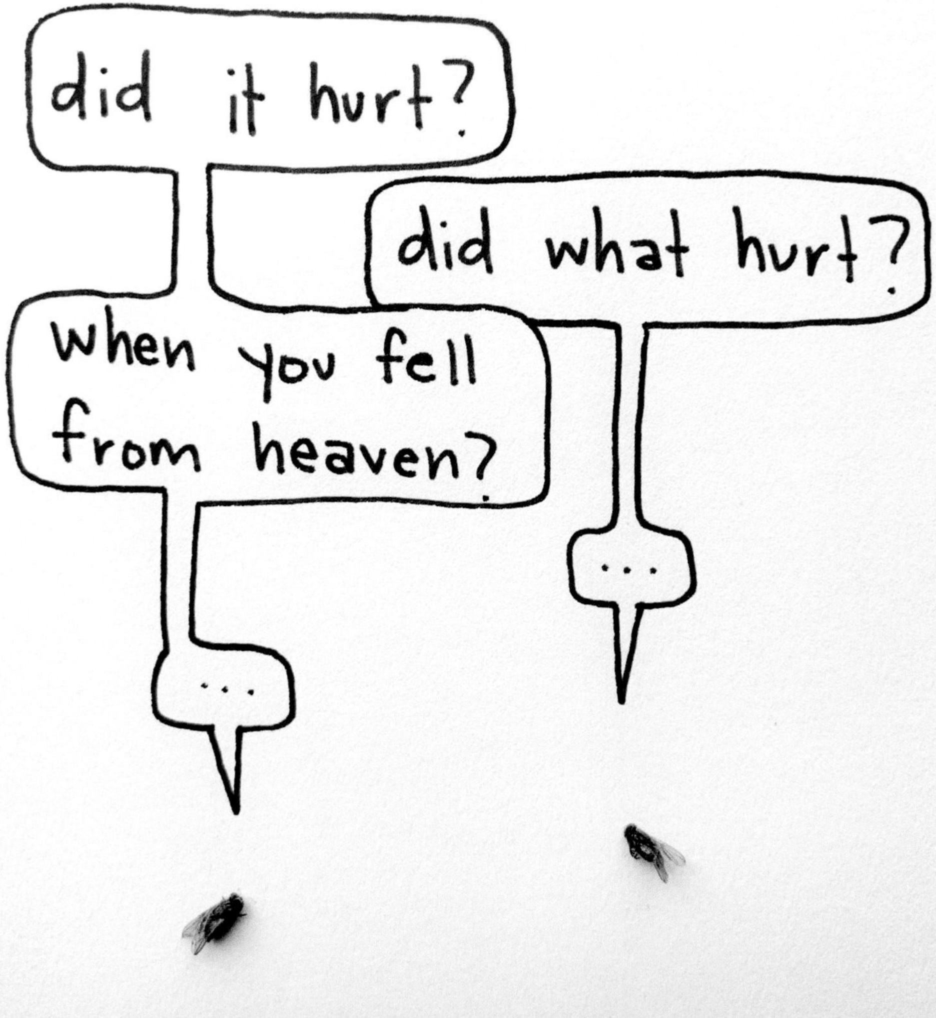

did it hurt?
did what hurt?
when you fell from heaven?
...
...

flies away

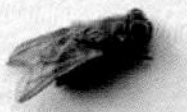

b

be

bee

Bees as in bee.

Born to fly.

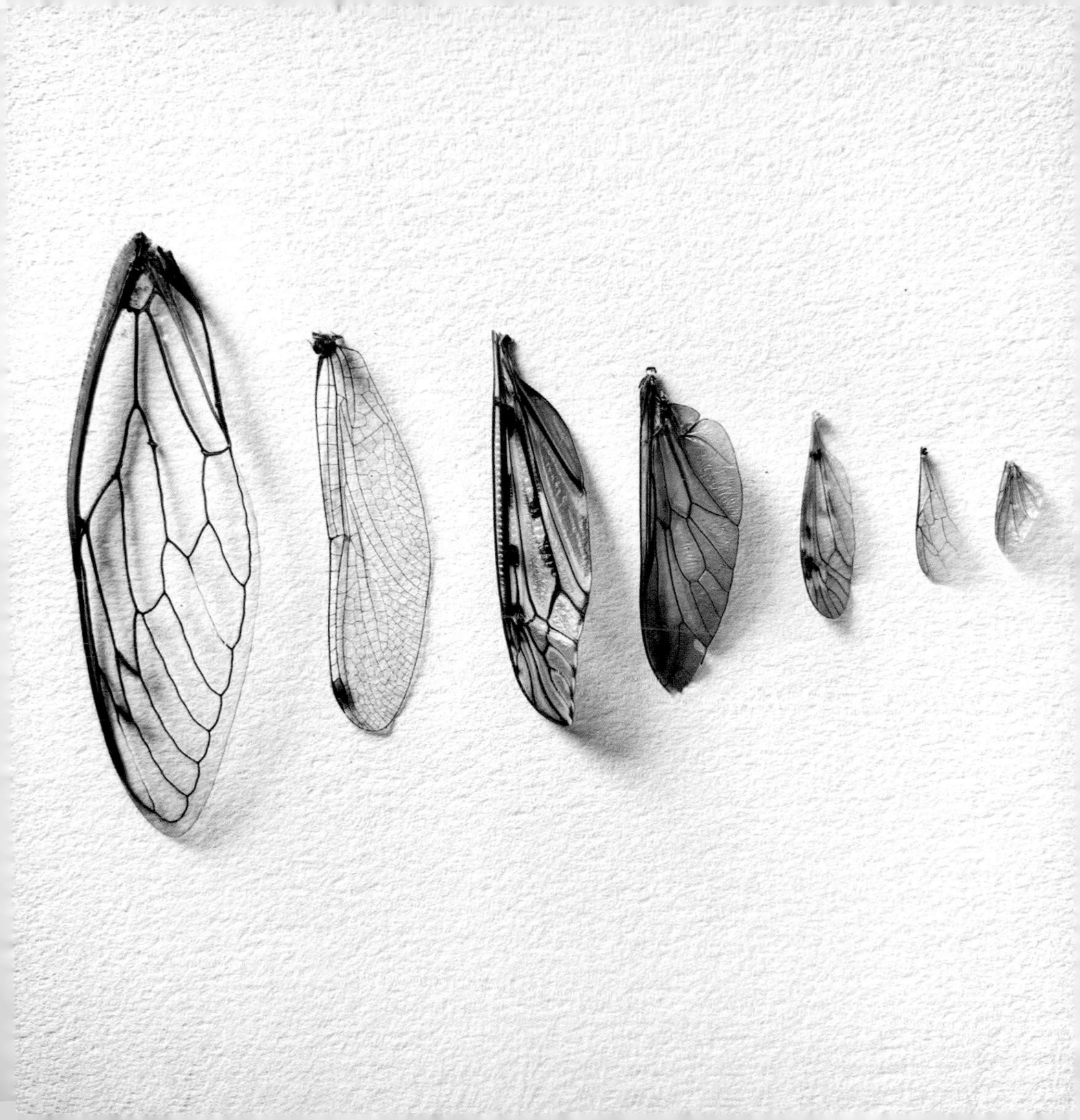

Time flies.

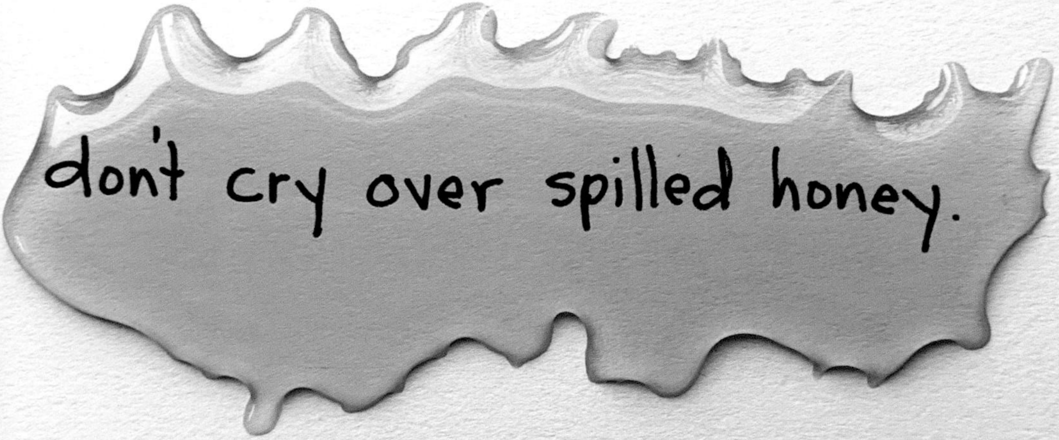
don't cry over spilled honey.

In fact, don't cry over spilled anything.

Metamorphosis or bust.

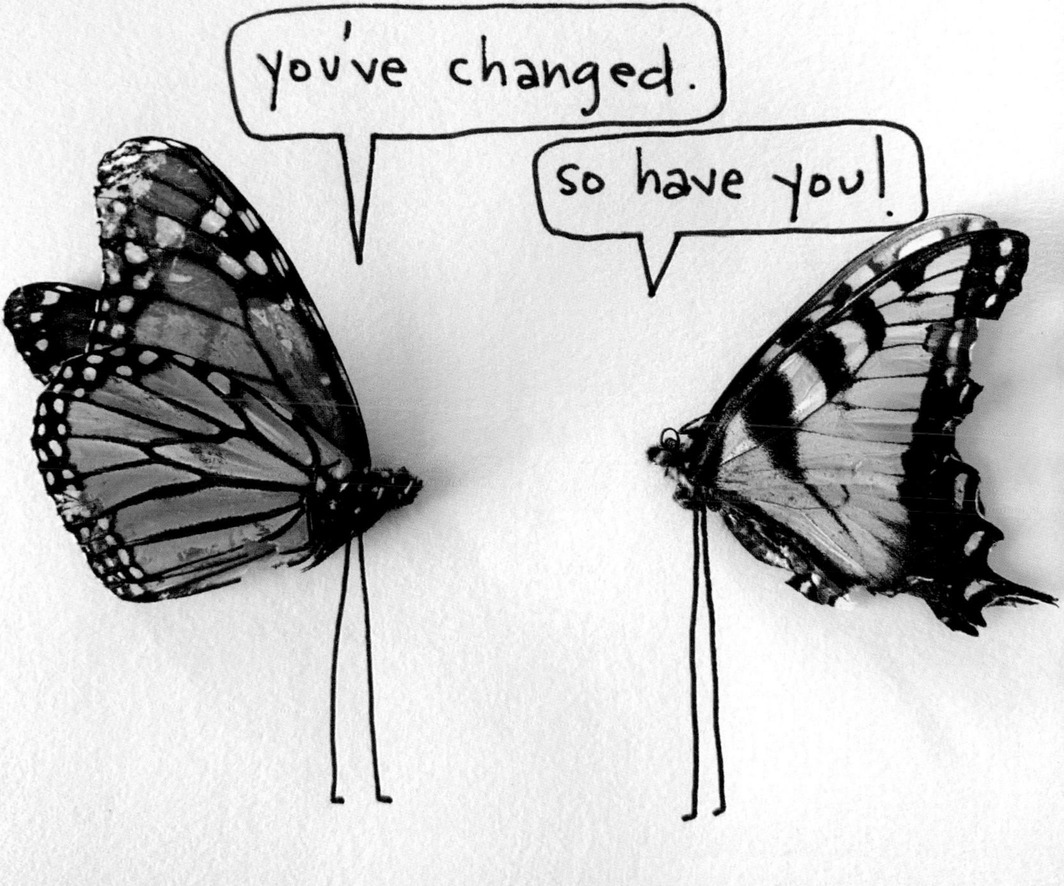
you've changed.
so have you!

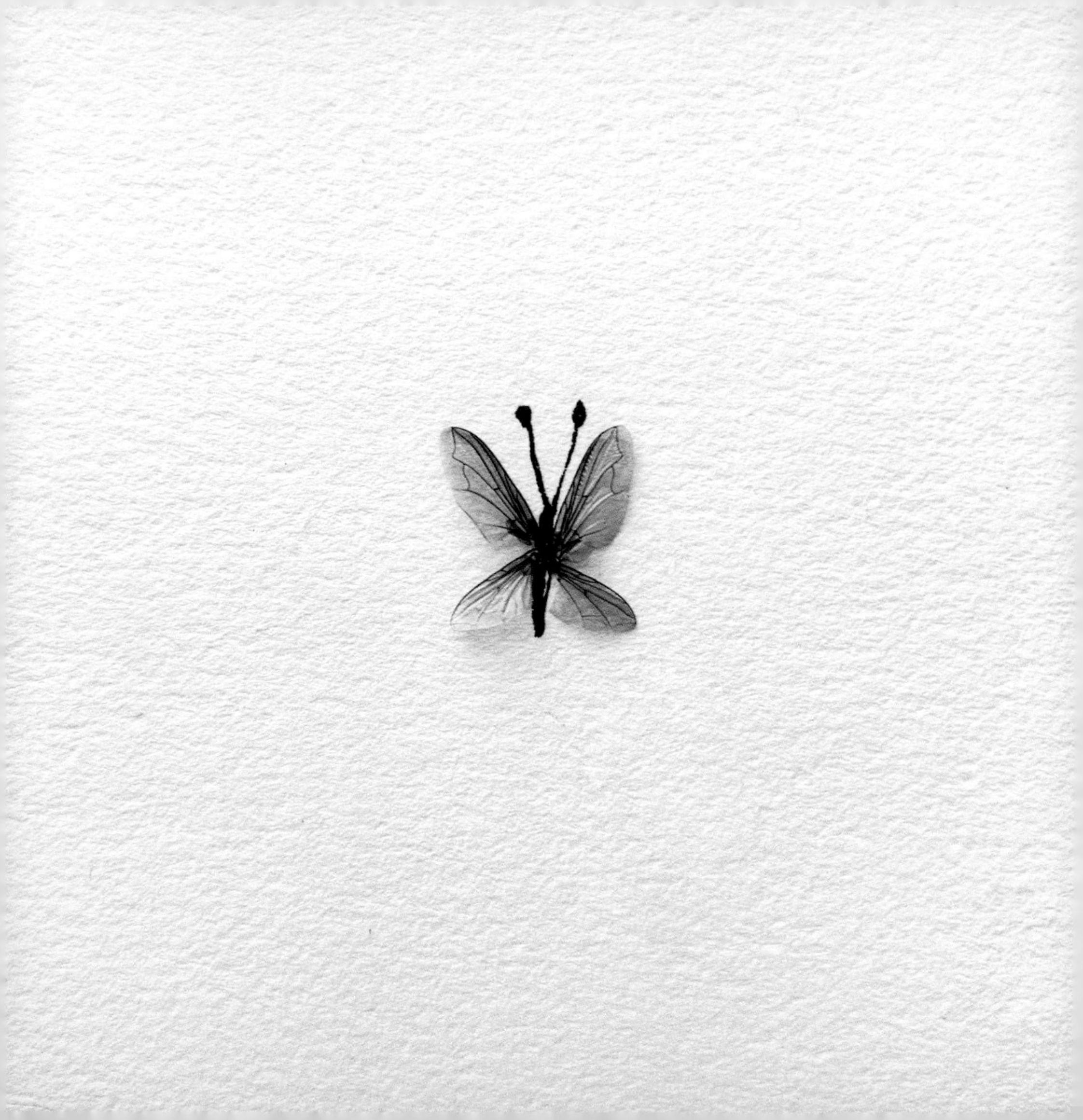

Butterfly fly.

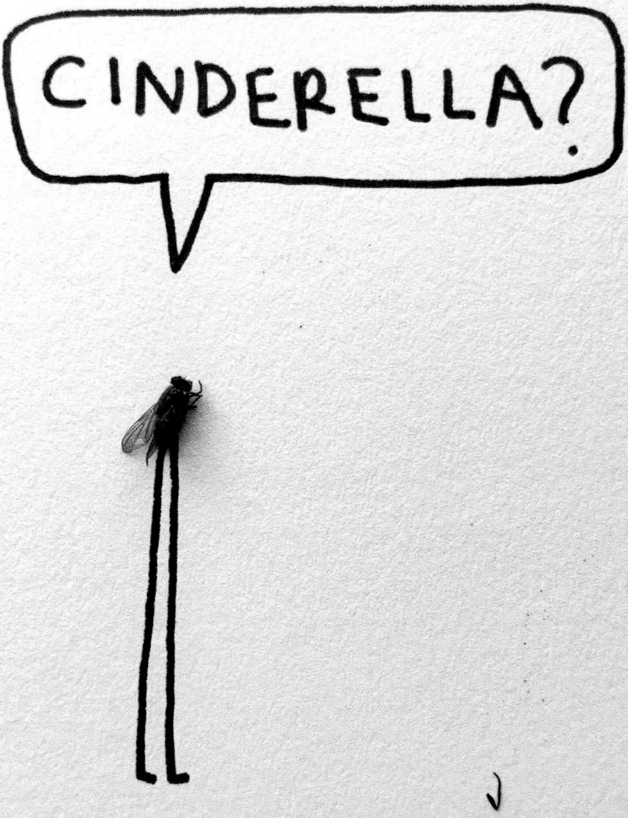
CINDERELLA?

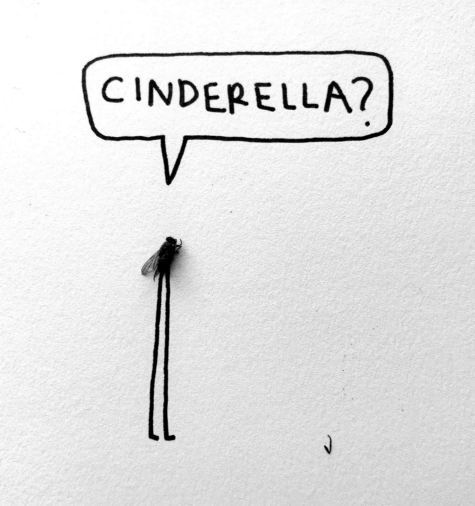

Prince Charming?

ladies, if he:
- never texts you back
- lives with a bunch of girls
- keeps searching for his
  "true queen"
- refuses to cook or clean
  for himself
- is a tiny drone

he's not your man. he is
a male bee.

men, if she:
- loves flowers
- cooks and cleans for you
- is too busy for drama

she's not your girl. she is
a worker bee.

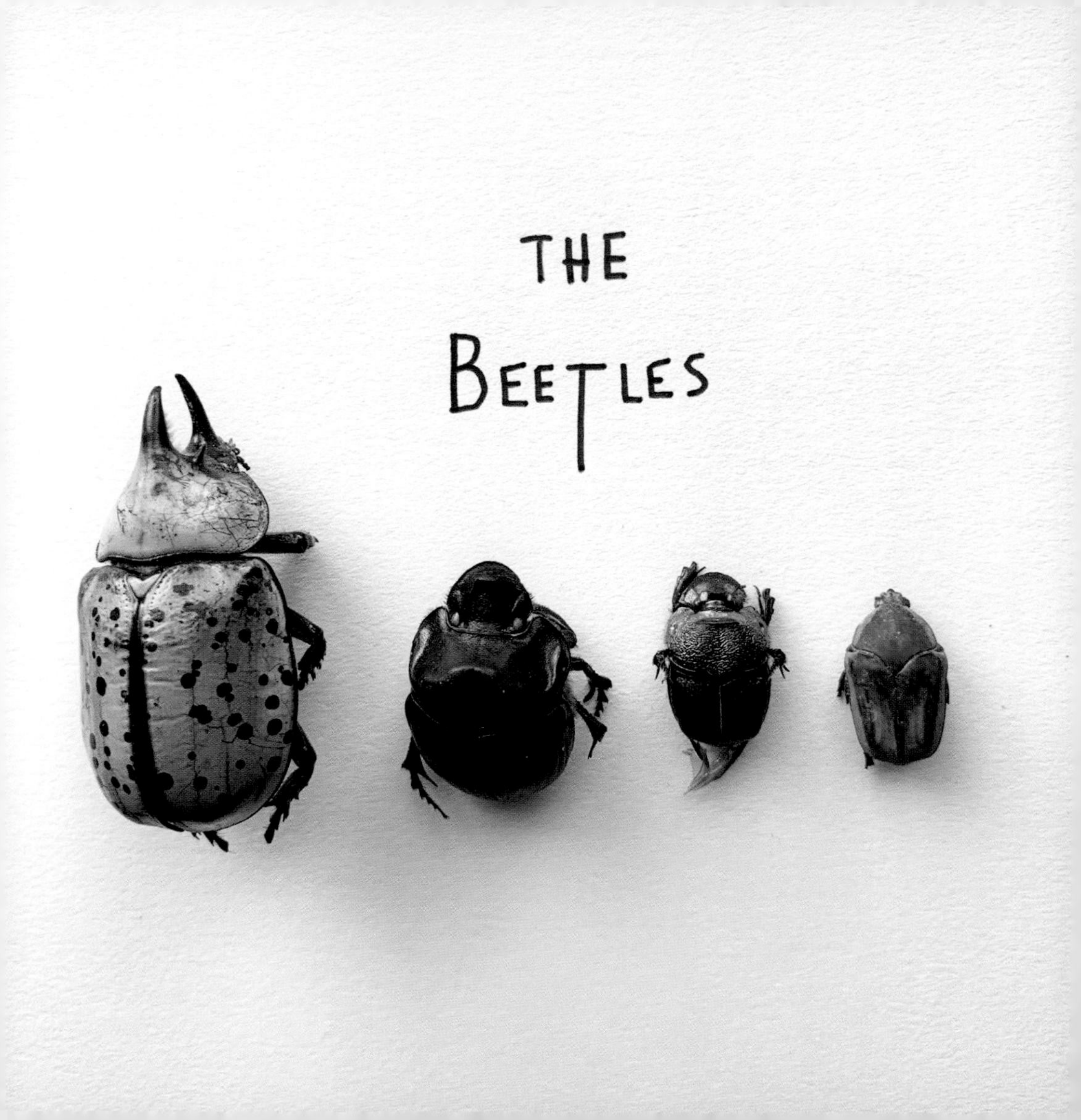
THE
BEETLES

It's been a hard day's night, and I've been working like a bug.

The moment you realize you overdressed for the party.

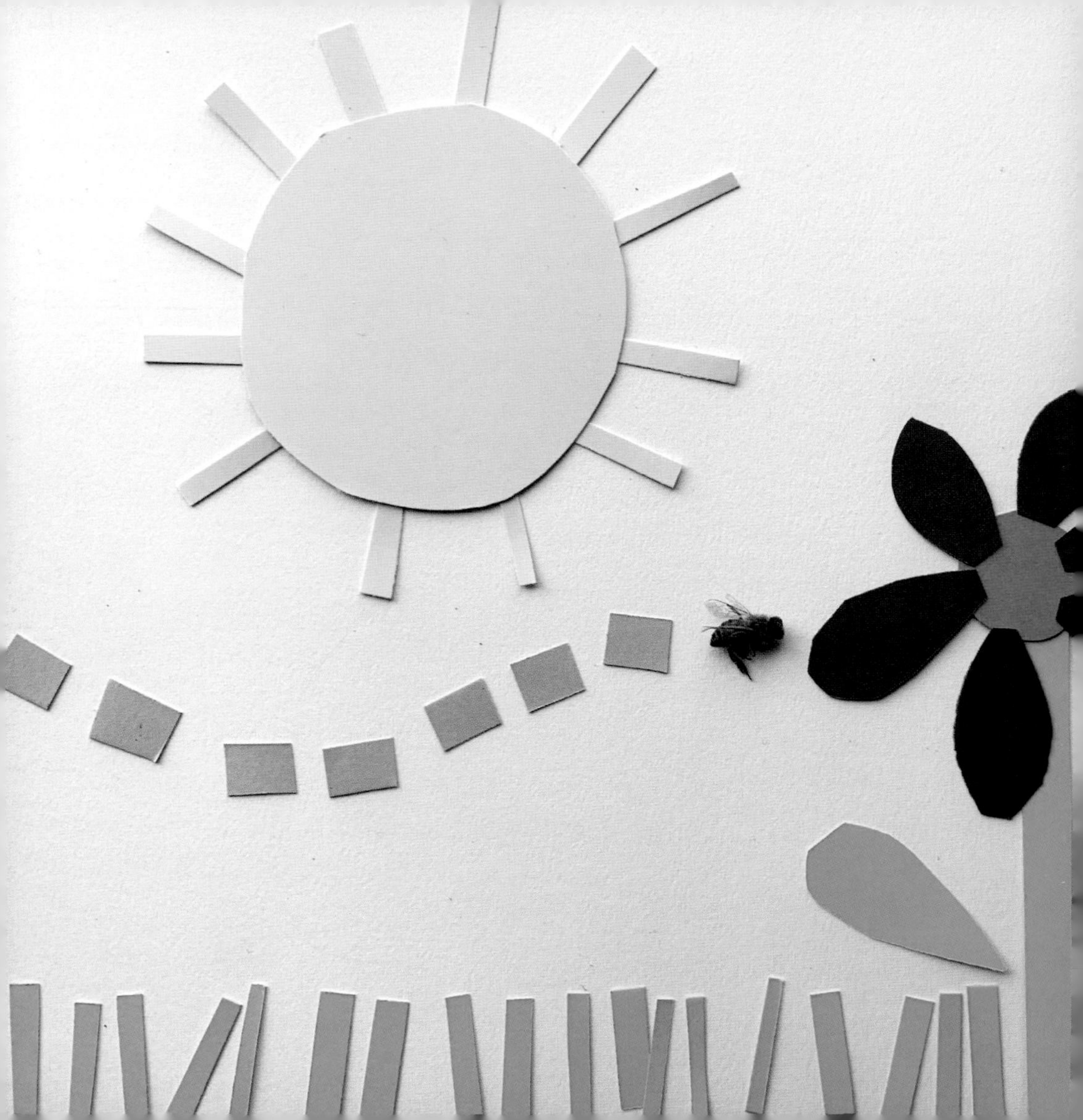

The female bee flies
an average of 375
miles in her lifetime.

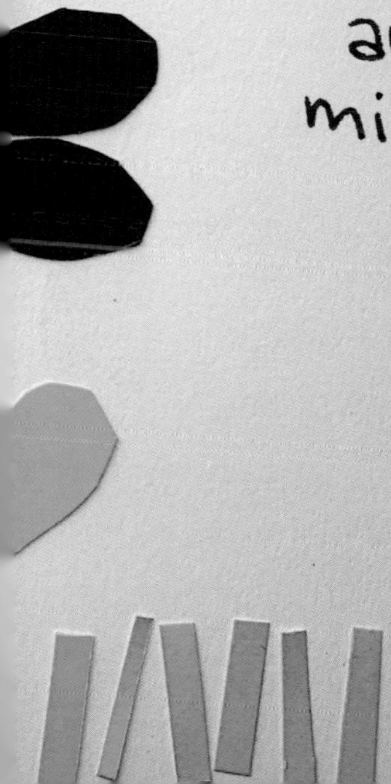

Mid-fly crisis.

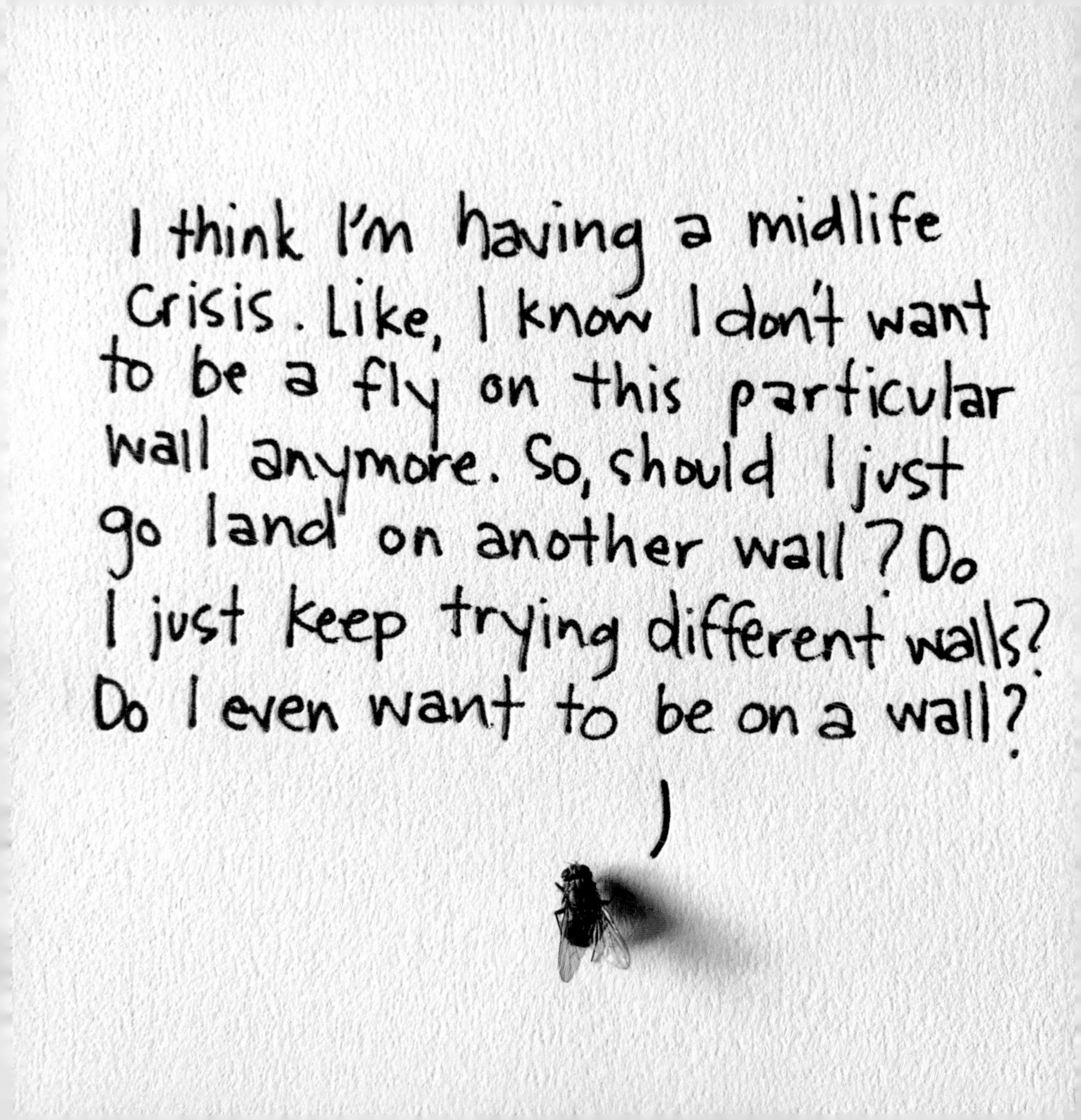
I think I'm having a midlife crisis. Like, I know I don't want to be a fly on this particular wall anymore. So, should I just go land on another wall? Do I just keep trying different walls? Do I even want to be on a wall?

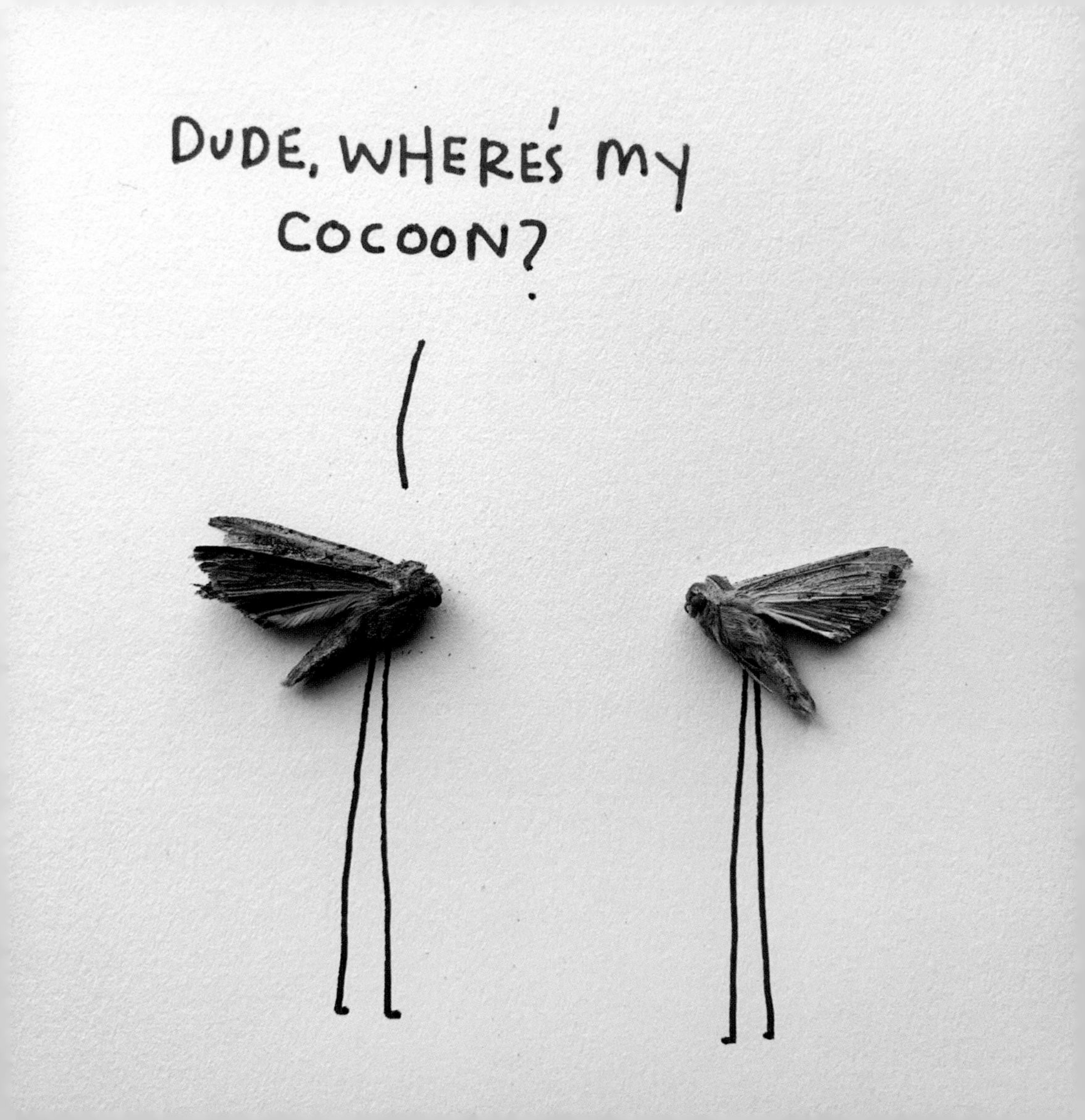
DUDE, WHERE'S MY COCOON?

Contrary to popular belief,
it is actually moths that make cocoons,
not butterflies.

Three easy steps for world domination.

BLOOM WHERE YOU
ARE PLANTED.
ATTRACT BUGS.
POLLINATE THE WORLD.

Ladybugs are a sign of good luck.
Here are forty-eight signs.

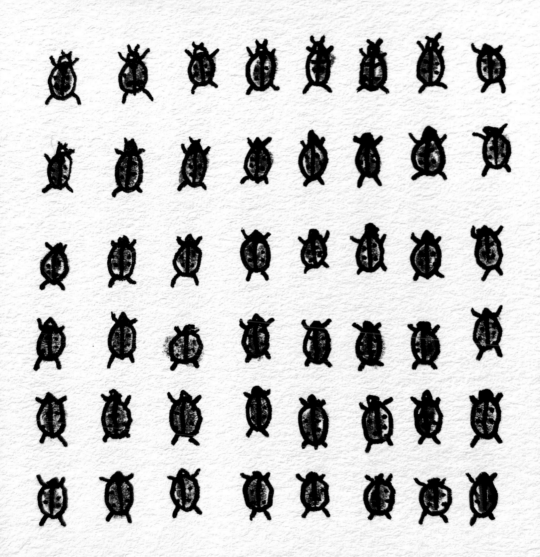

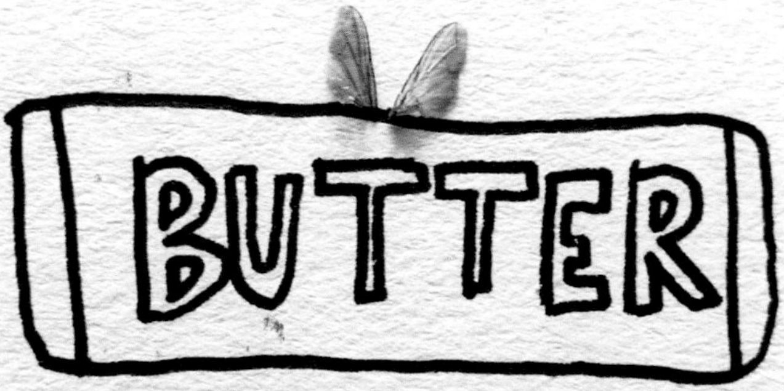
BUTTER

Flying butter.

I am exactly where I need to be.

I AM EXACTLY WHERE I NEEDED TO .

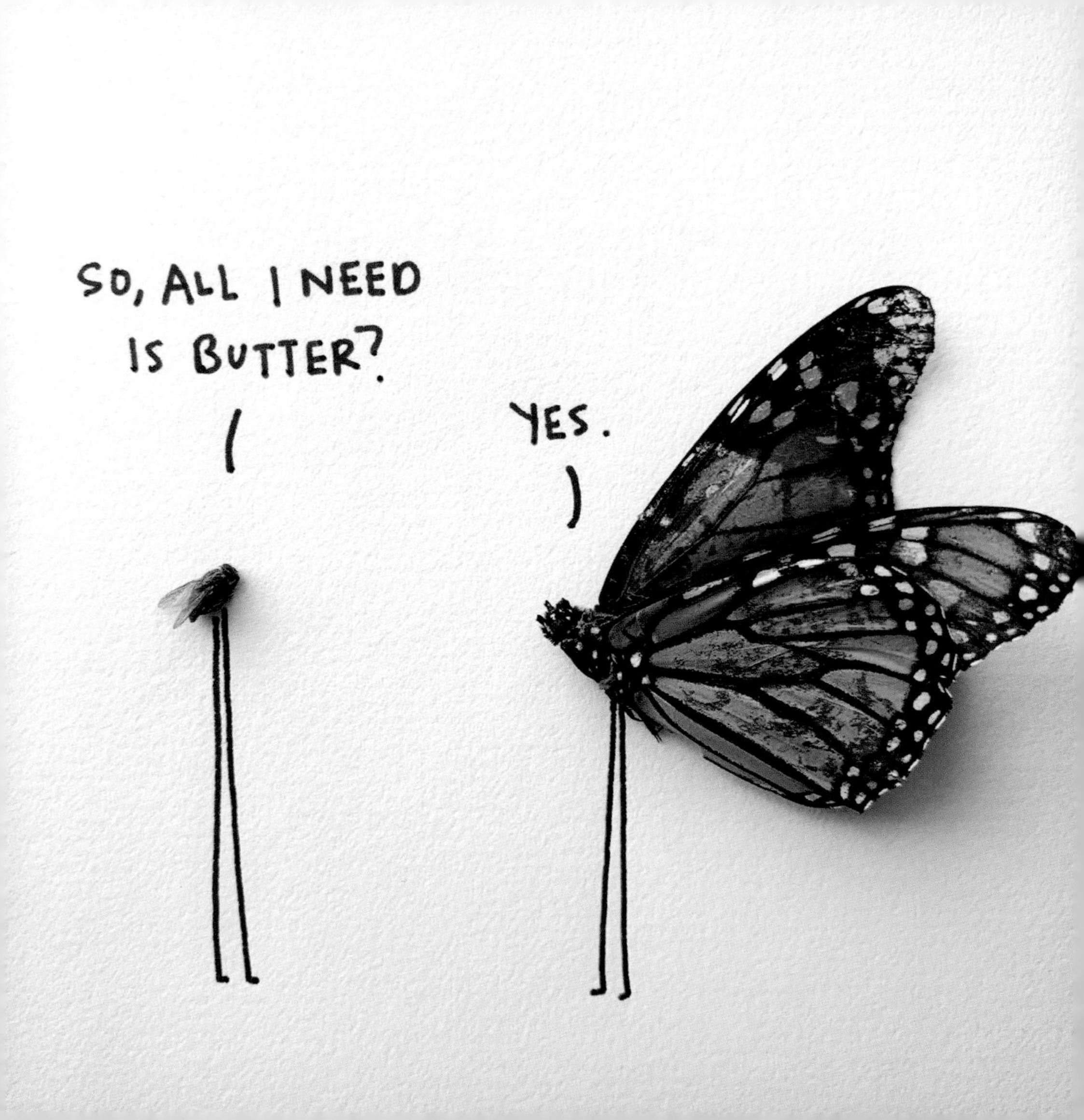
SO, ALL I NEED IS BUTTER?
YES.

goes to store to buy a shitload of butter

Please consult your doctor before attempting the chrysalis method.

THE CHRYSALIS METHOD

1. FIND SECLUSION
2. BREAK YOURSELF DOWN SO YOU BECOME A PILE OF PURE NOTHINGNESS
3. WHILE REMAINING IN SOLITUDE, SLOWLY PIECE YOURSELF BACK TOGETHER
4. EMERGE INTO THE WORLD COMPLETELY TRANSFORMED

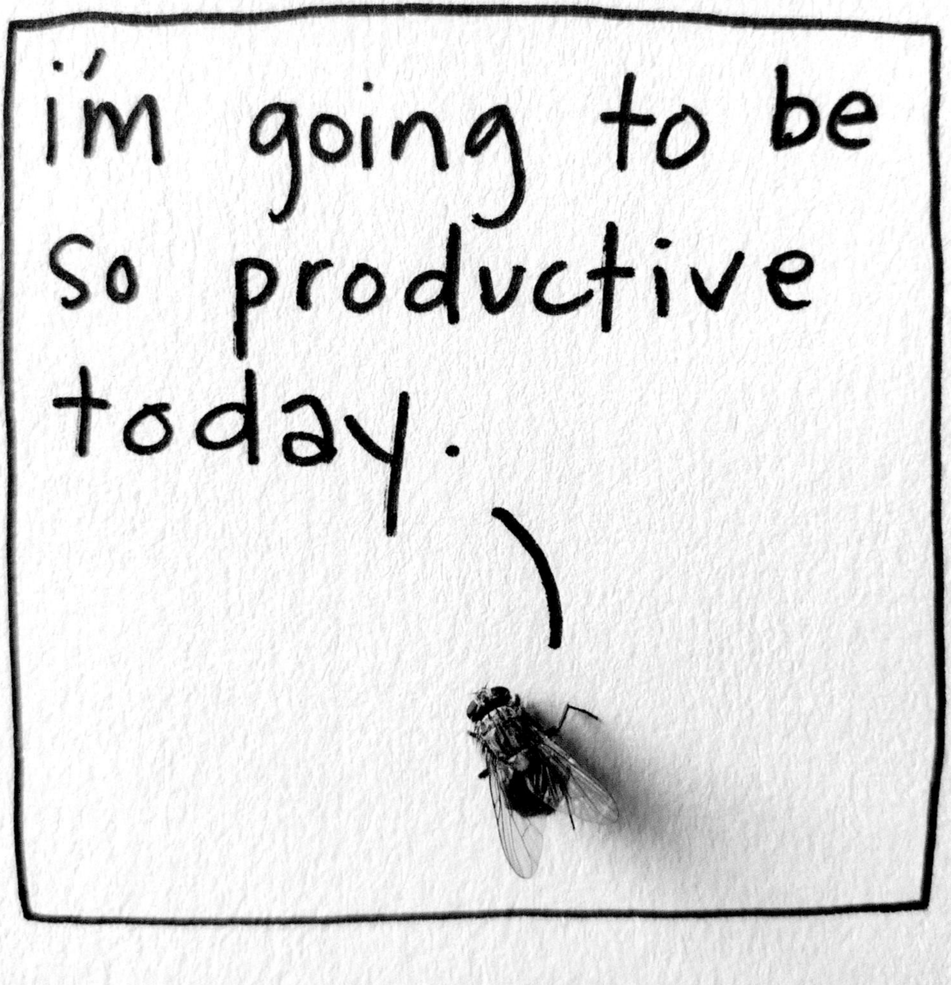
i'm going to be so productive today.

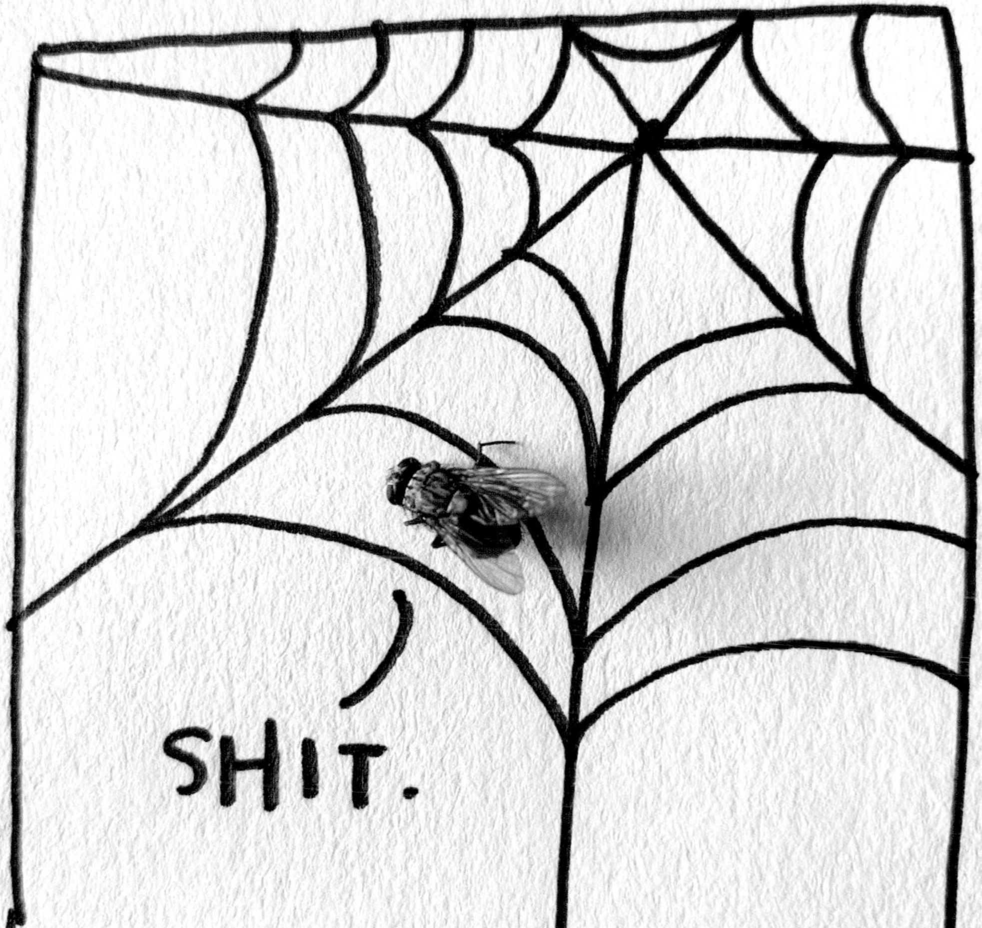
SHIT.

Okay, greeting card company,
but make it spider.

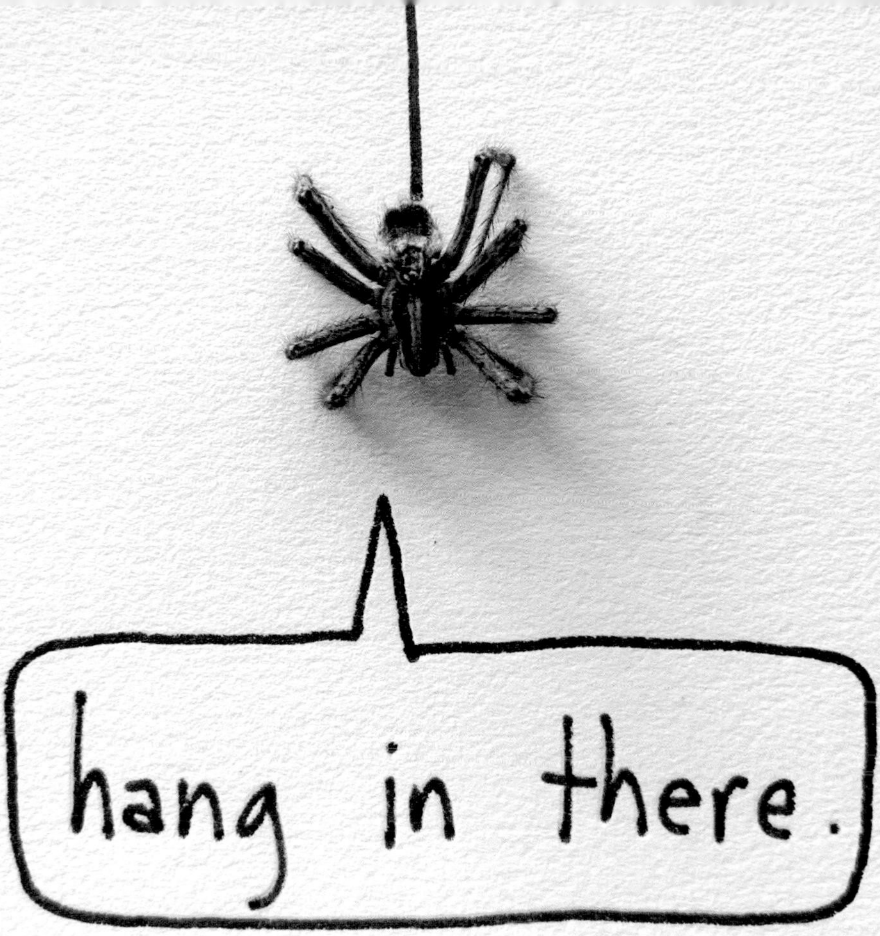
hang in there.

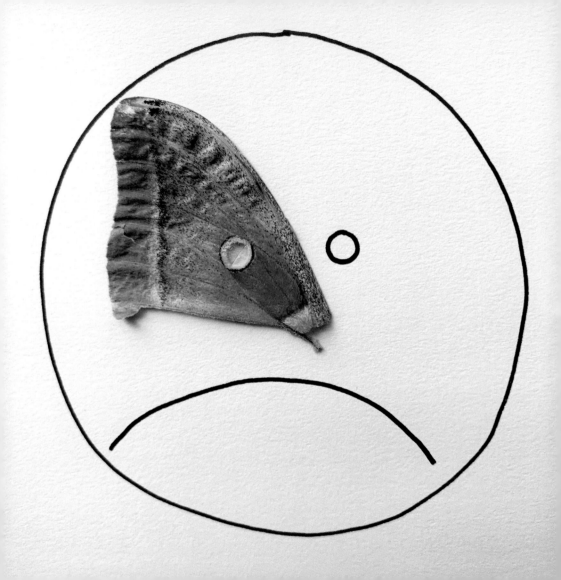

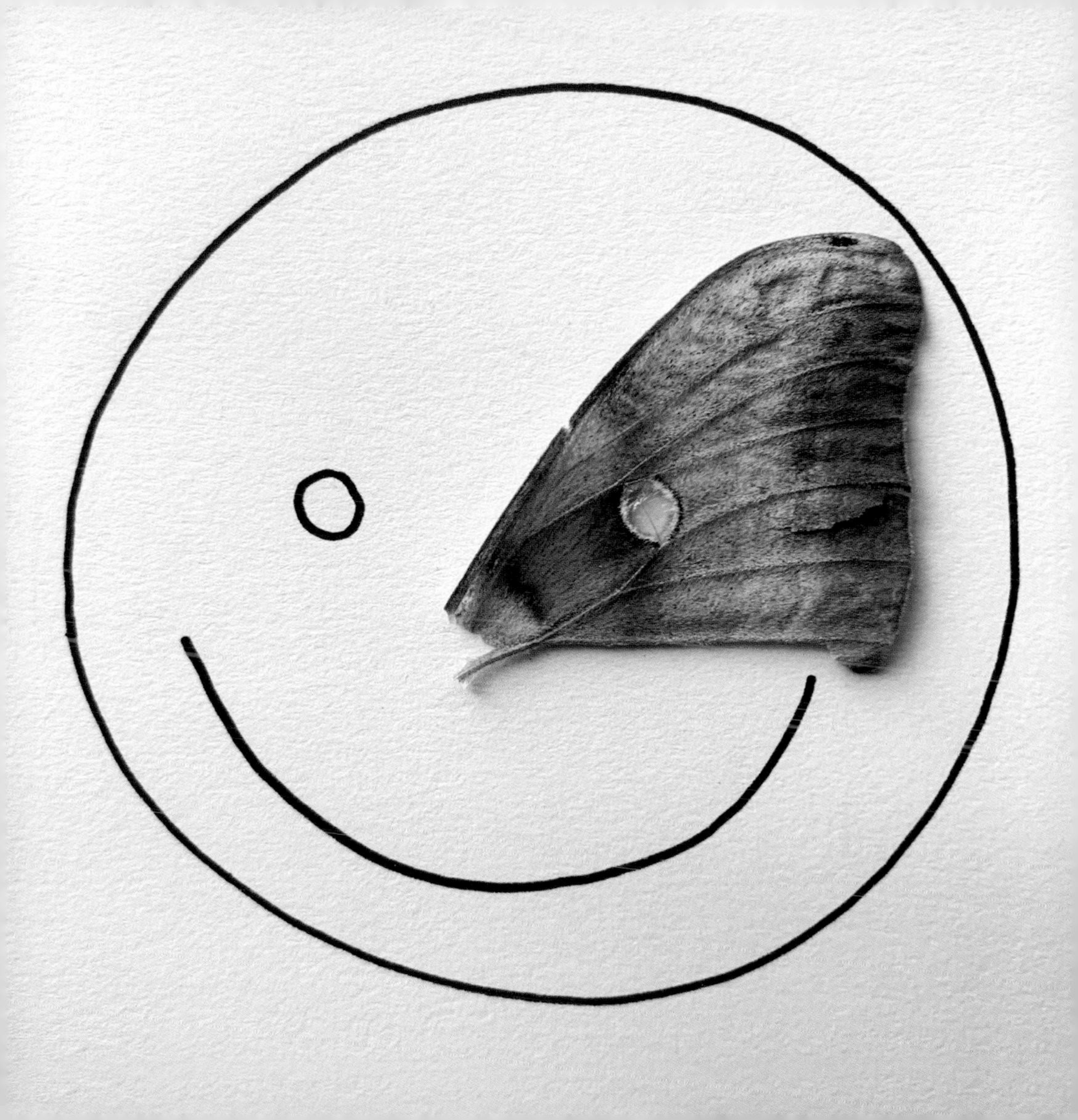

Litterbugs are the worst kind of bugs.

DON'T BE A
LITTERBUG,
BE A
LEAVE THE
PLANET
IN BETTER SHAPE
THAN YOU
FOUND IT BUG.

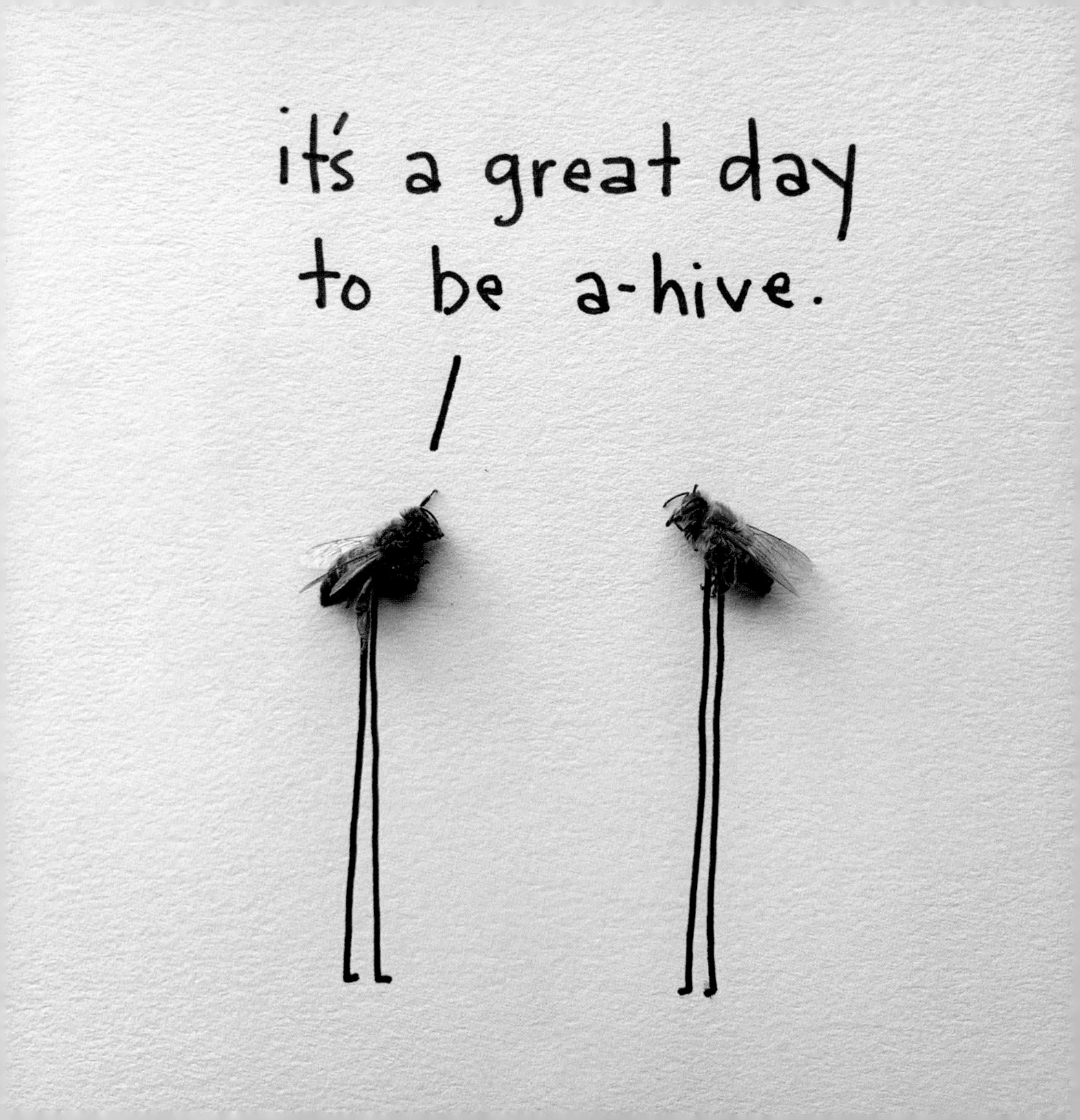
it's a great day
to be a-hive.

And also alive!

A short story about a rude snail.

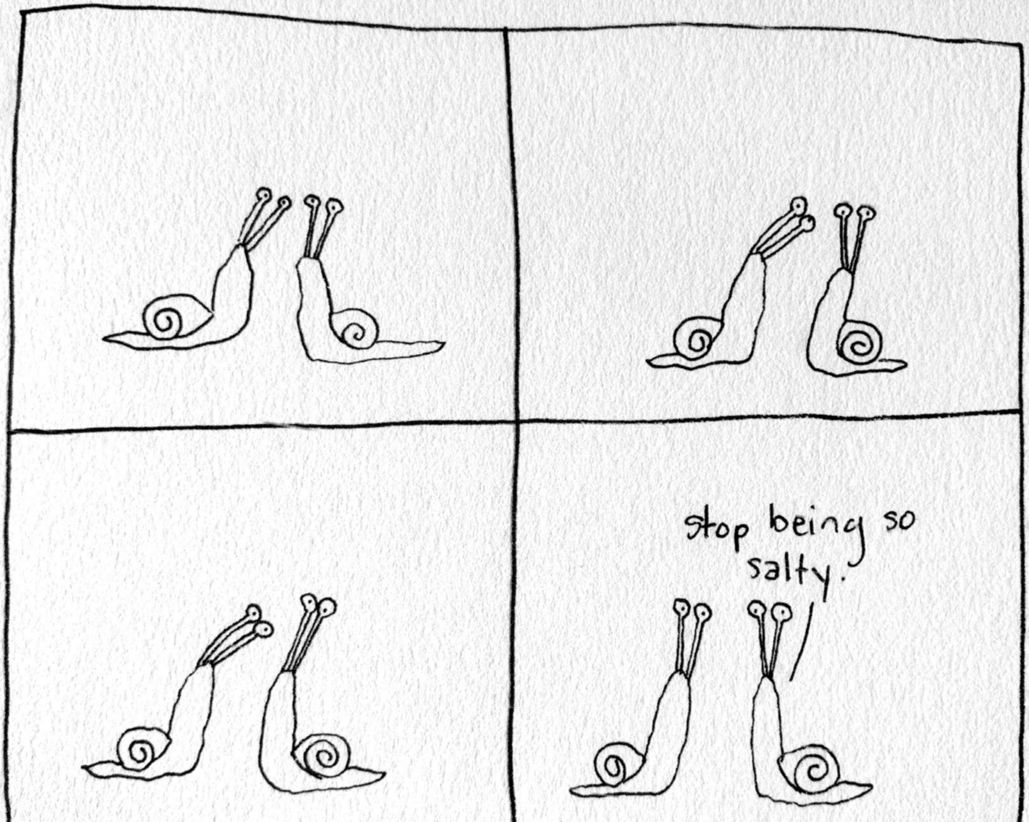
stop being so salty.

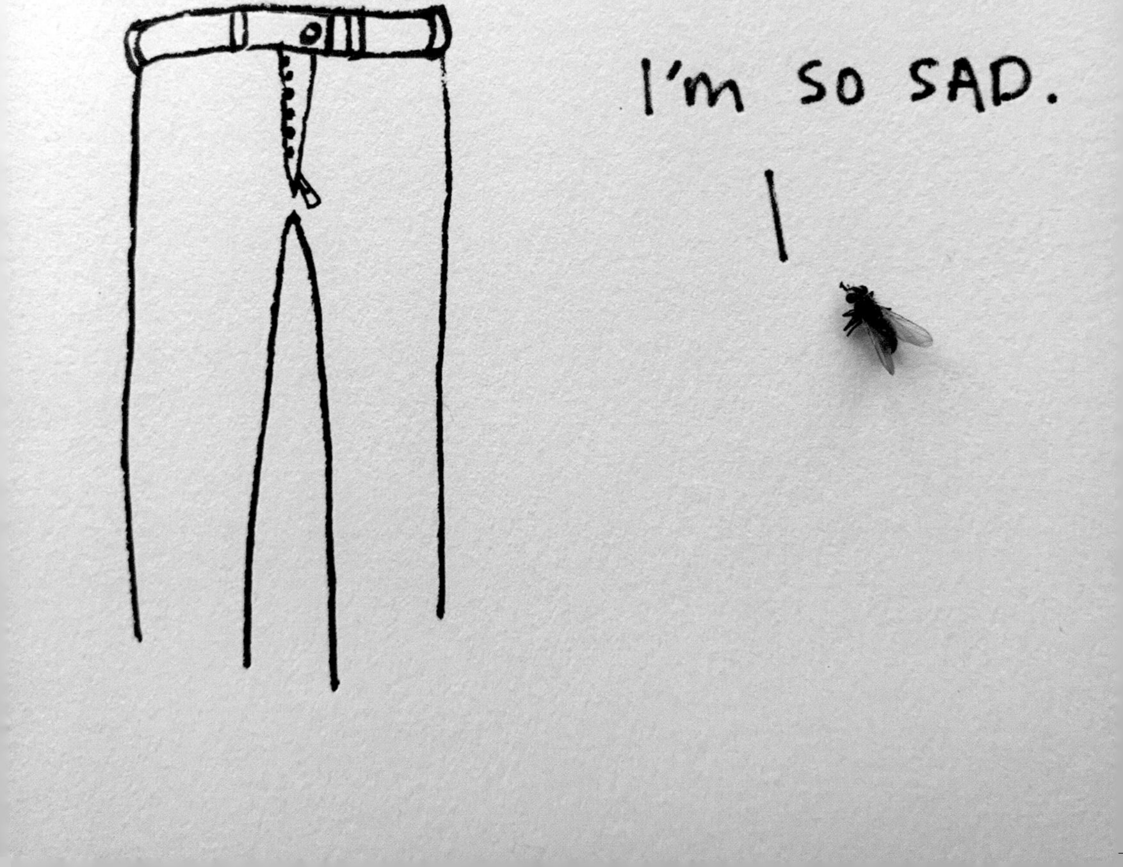
I'm so SAD.

When your flies are down.

Here is a free eye exam.

E
FP
T Z
LZED
PECFD
EDFCZP

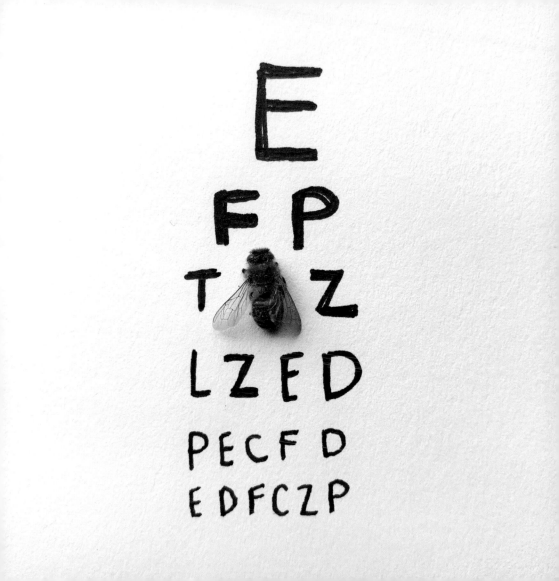

Meeting someone on the web like . . .

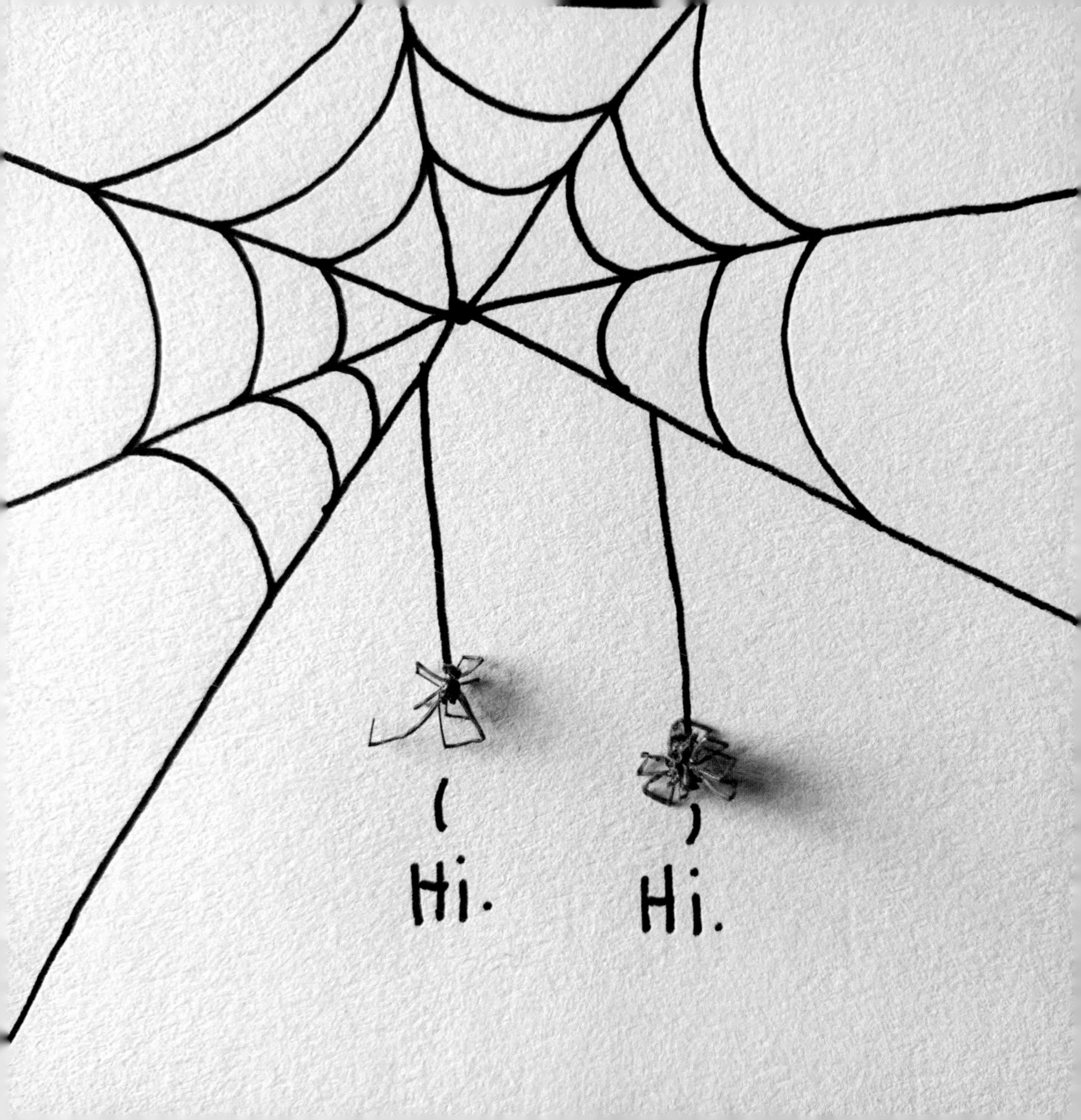
Hi.
Hi.

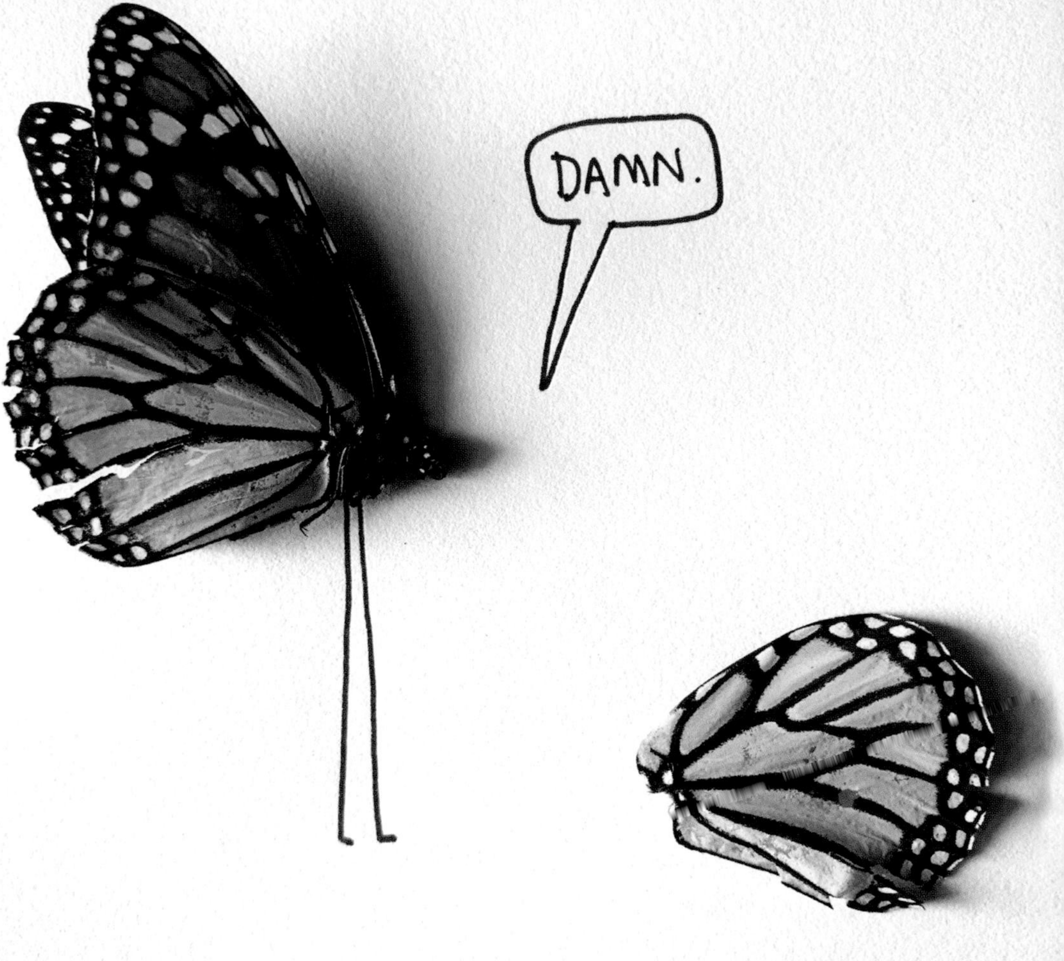
DAMN.

I'm fine, it's fine, everything is fine.

you fly away.
no, you fly away.
no, you.
no, you.
let's fly away at the same time.
okay.

Love is flying away at the same time.

Insects are friends!

I N S E C T O S

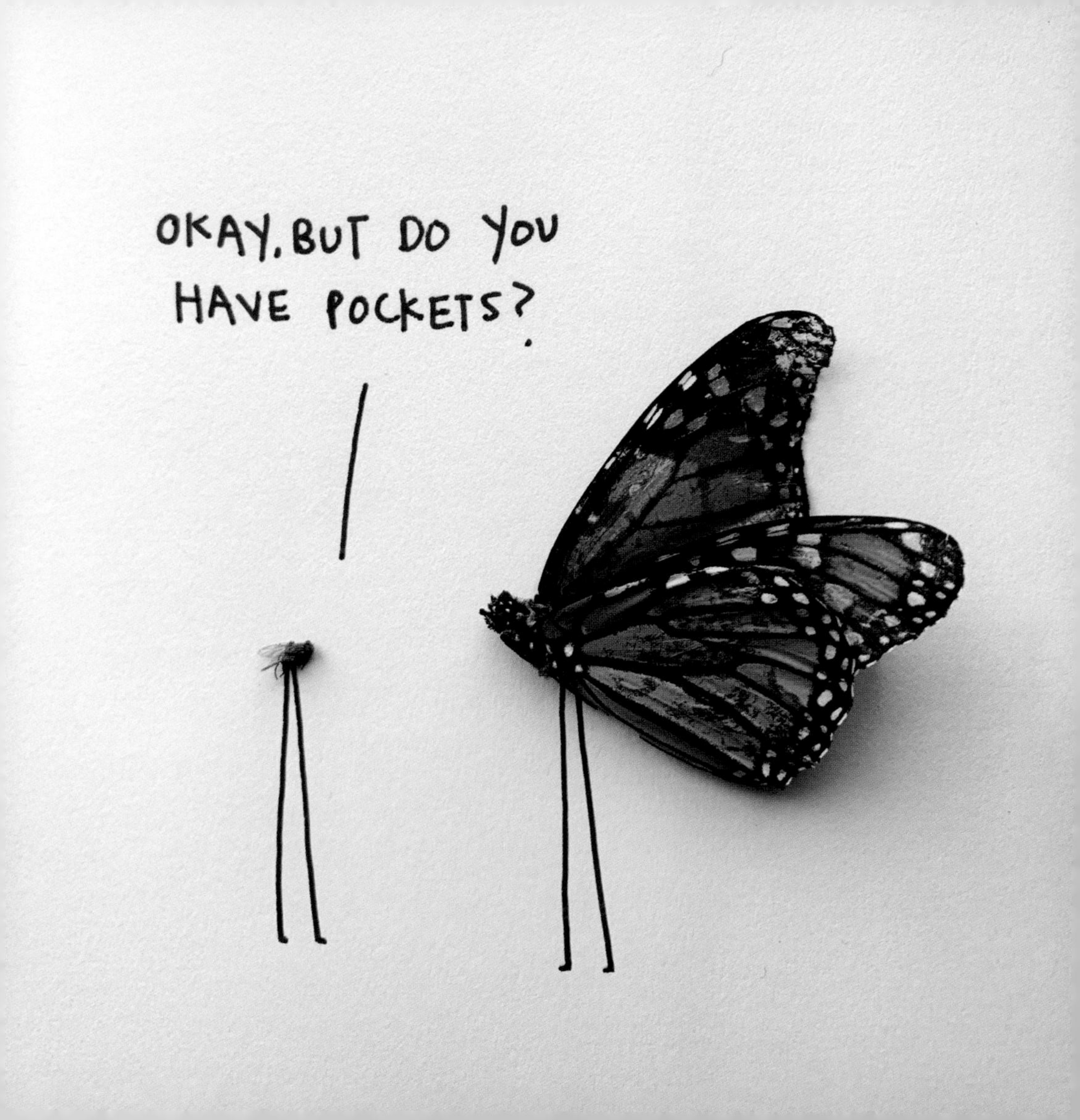
OKAY, BUT DO YOU
HAVE POCKETS?

I'll pay top dollar for some pockets.

Who runs the world?

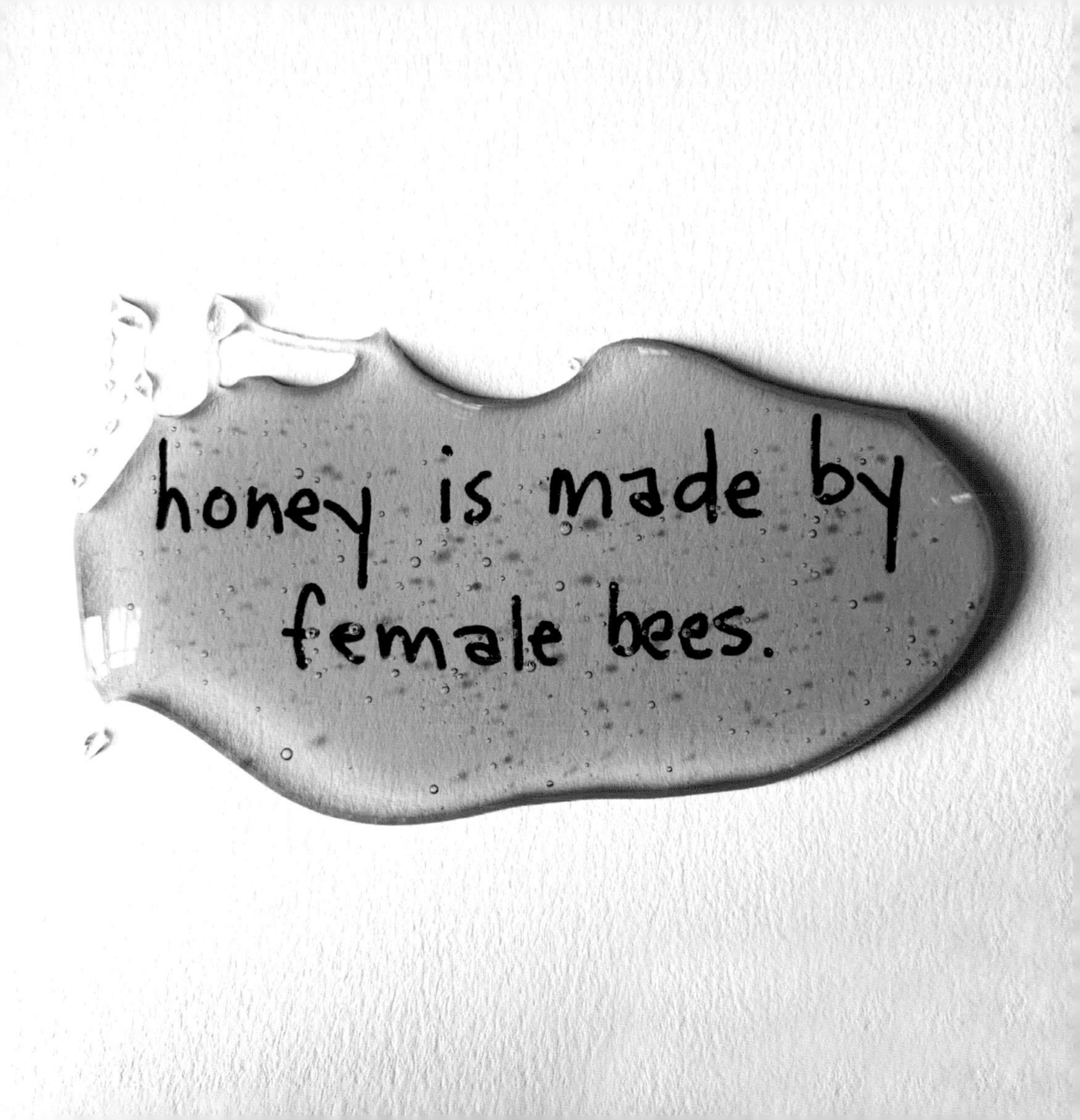
honey is made by
female bees.

adjusts butterfly antenna

Wink.

Repeat after me.

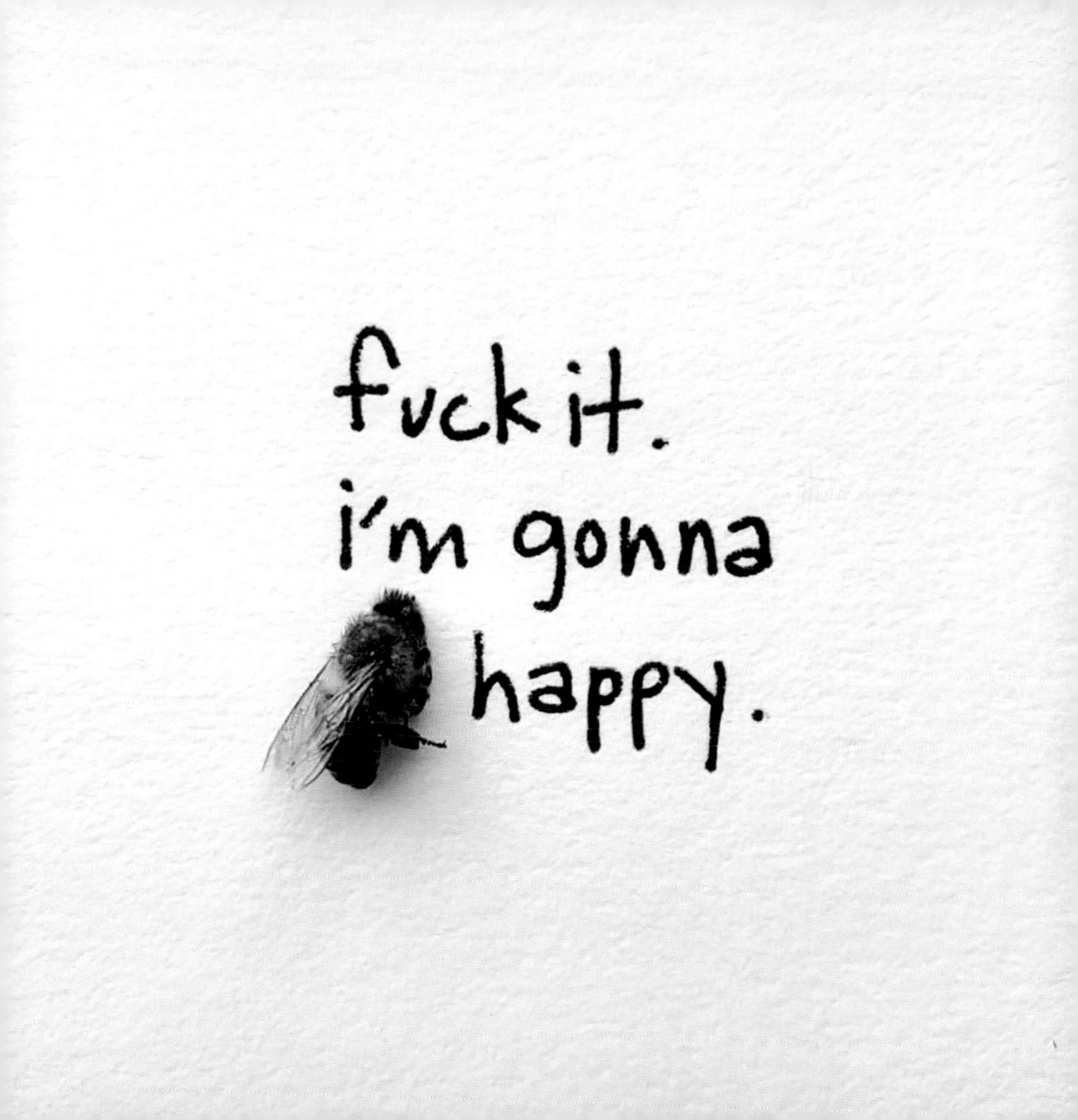
fuck it.
i'm gonna
happy.

do you want to go make out in a garbage can?
i love it when you talk dirty to me.

My love language.

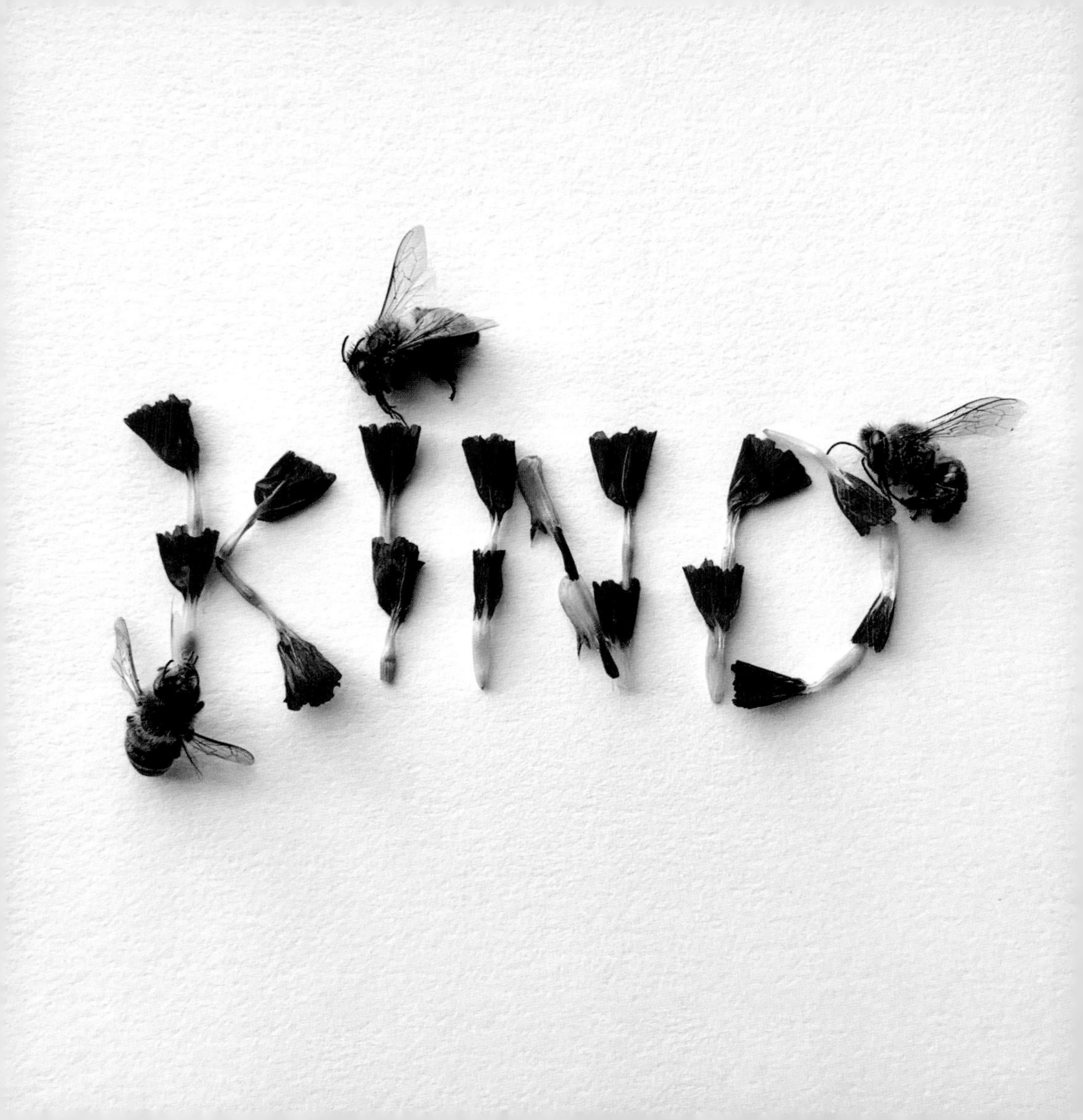
kind

To yourself.

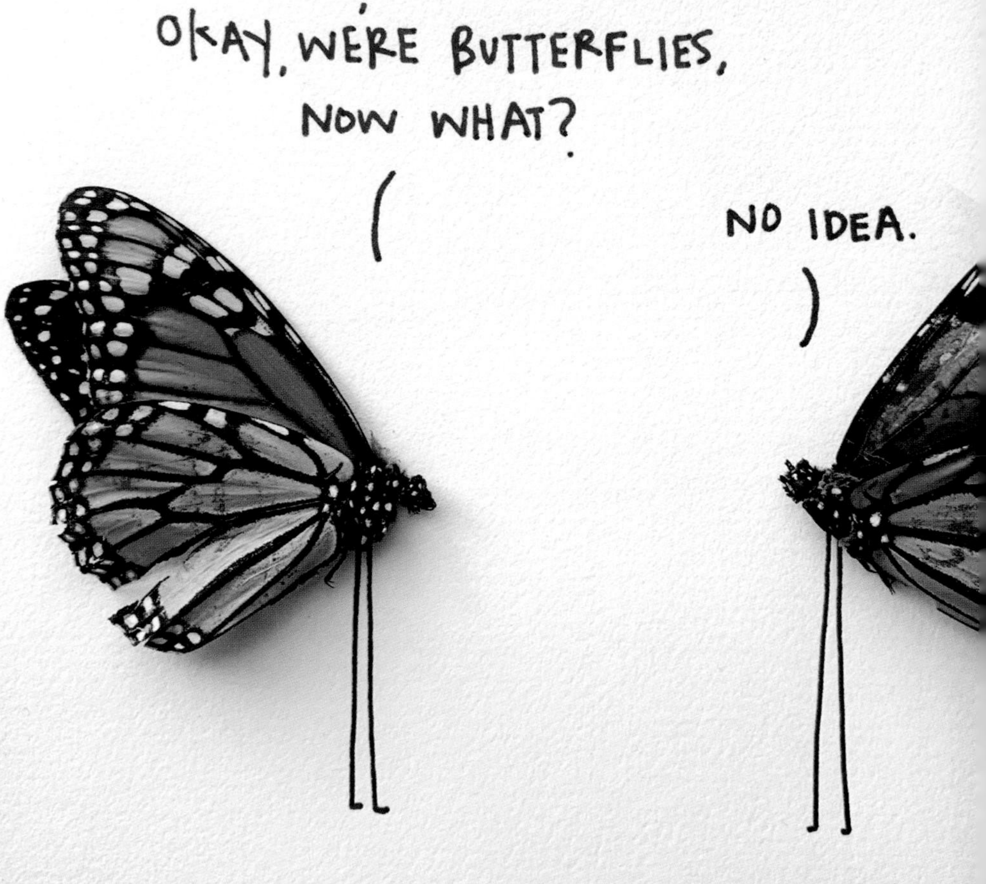

OKAY, WE'RE BUTTERFLIES, NOW WHAT?
NO IDEA.

Don't wish your life away.

make a wish.

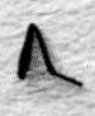

If you make a wish on a fly leg,
your wish will absolutely come true.
It's science.

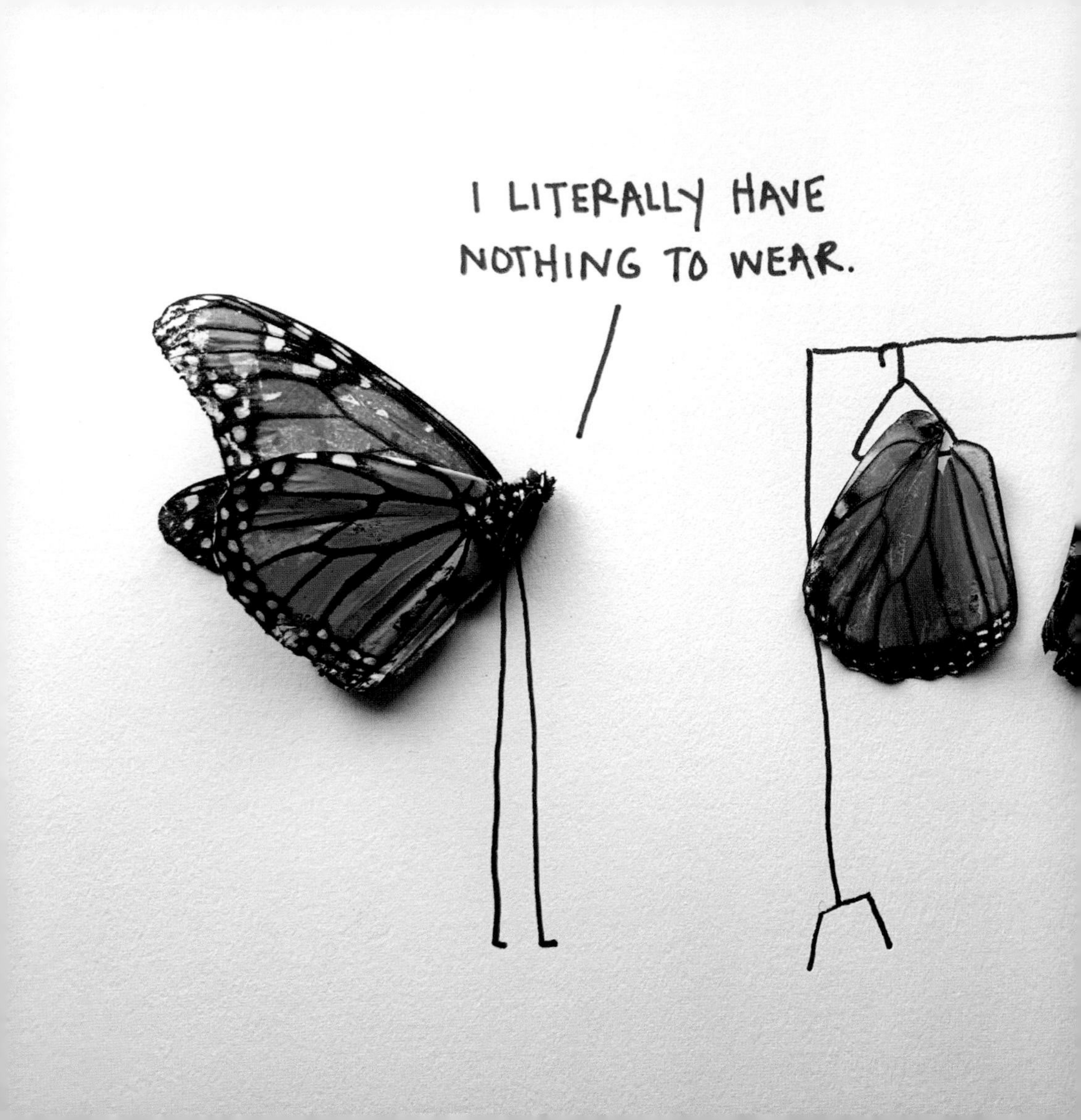
I LITERALLY HAVE NOTHING TO WEAR.

That moment when
your entire closet
looks the same.

Yum.

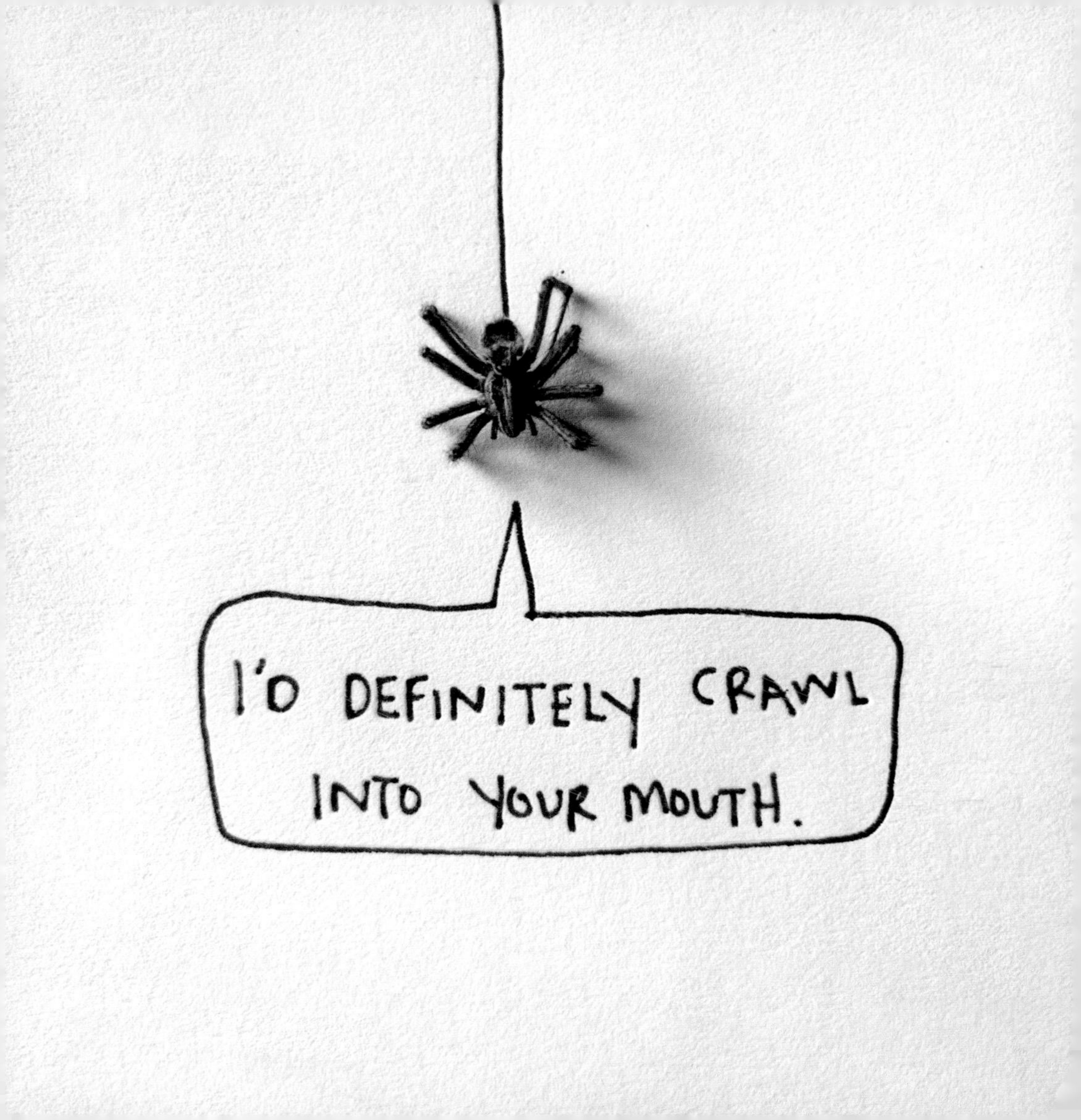
I'D DEFINITELY CRAWL INTO YOUR MOUTH.

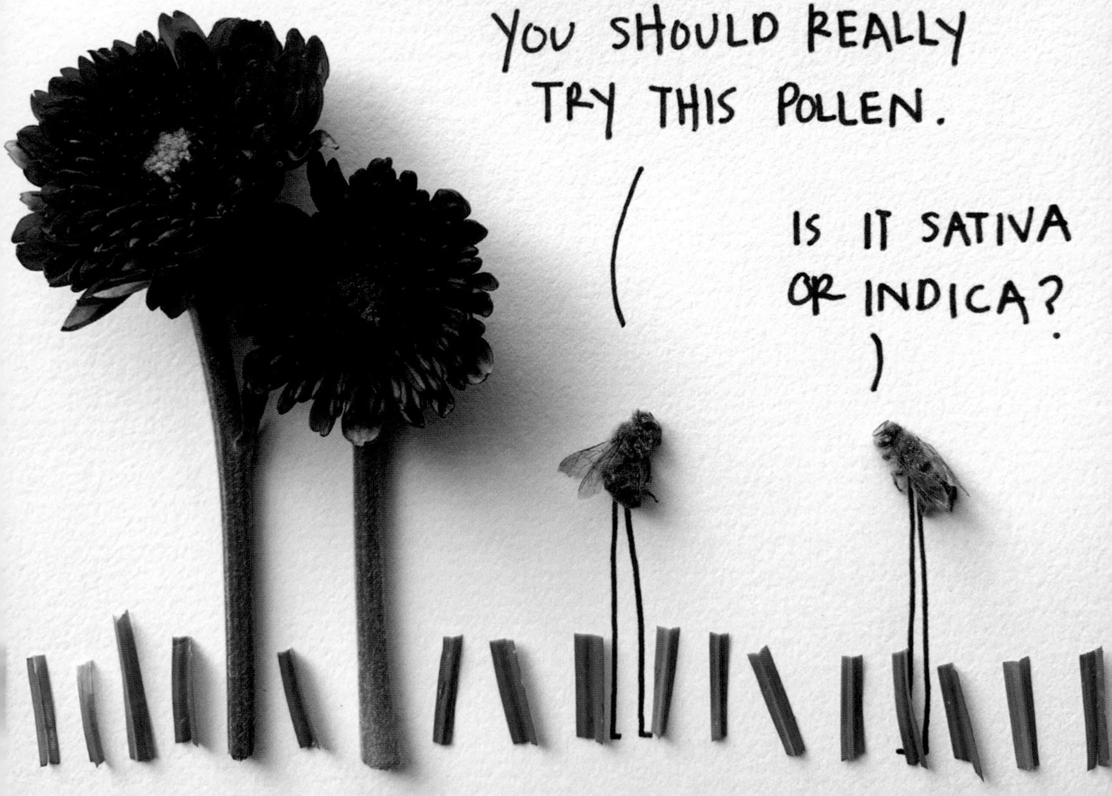
YOU SHOULD REALLY TRY THIS POLLEN.
IS IT SATIVA OR INDICA?

Indica and you're in da couch.

Arachnophobia knows no bounds.

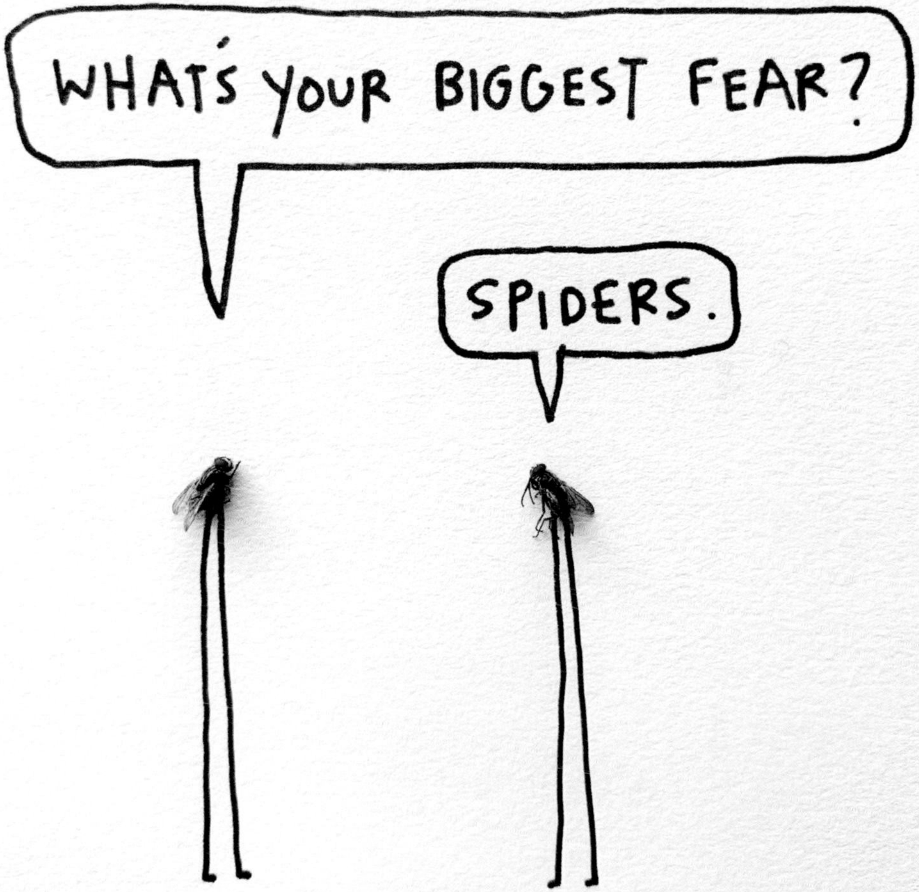
WHAT'S YOUR BIGGEST FEAR?
SPIDERS.

Dragon + fly = dragonfly

This is a positive phototaxis joke.

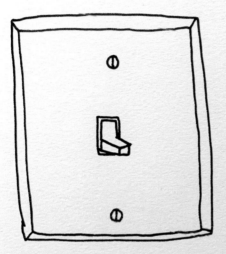

CAN I TURN
YOU ON?

we go together

like peanut butter and honey.

PB&H is the new PB&J.

Anyone over thirty will understand this.

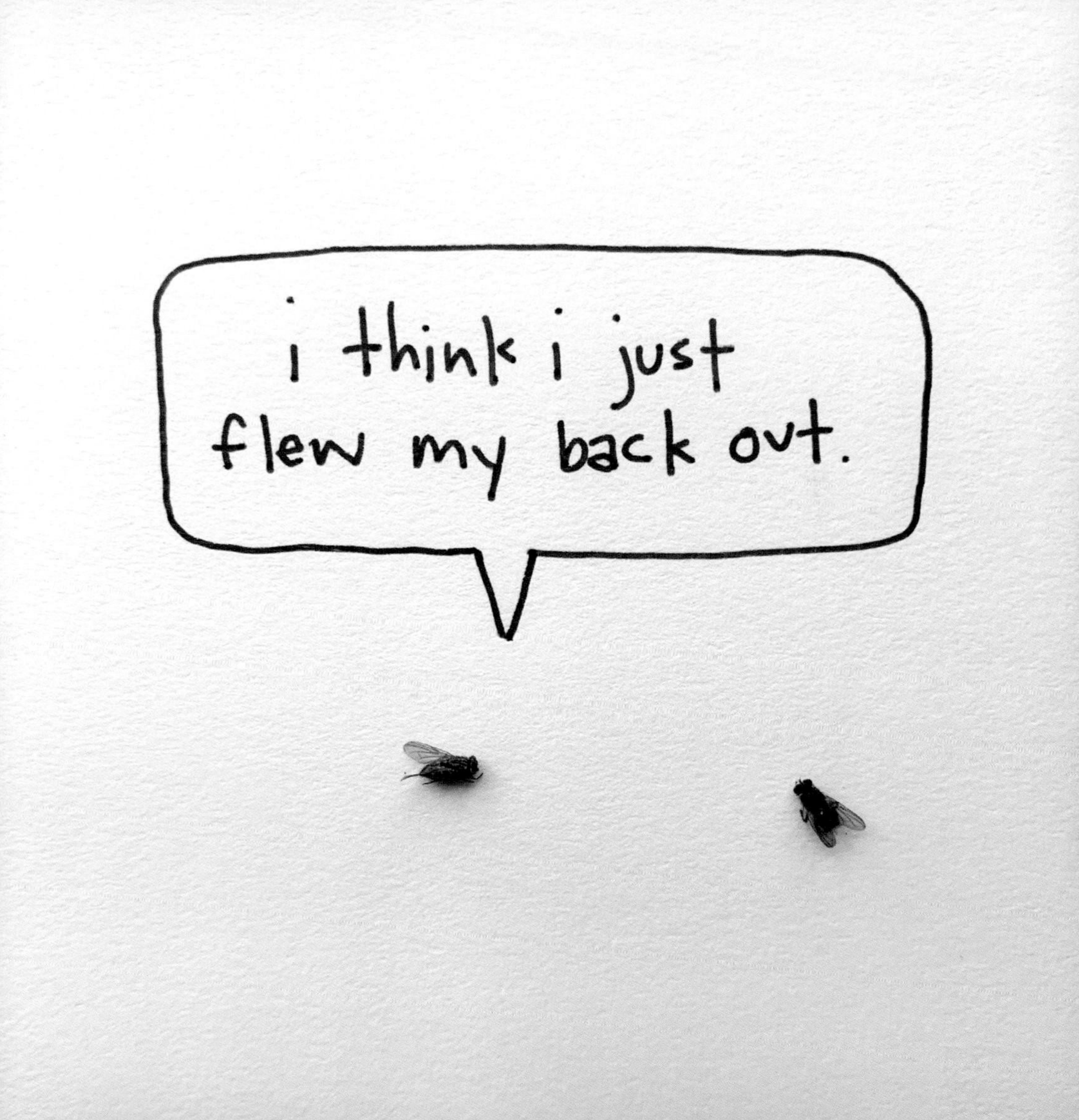
i think i just flew my back out.

Self-portrait.

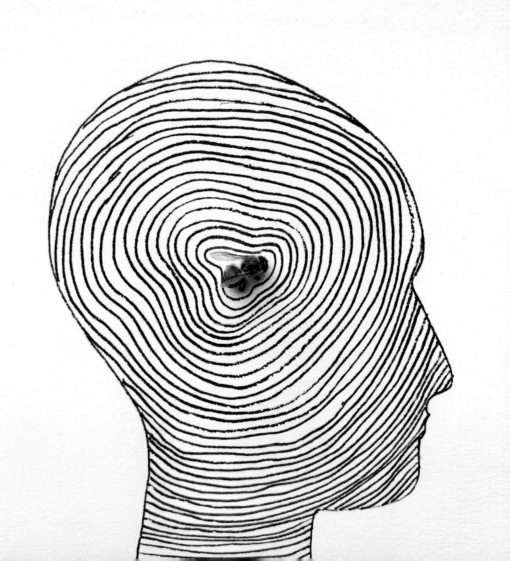

Do you think butterflies get butterflies?

THERE'S A FLUTTERING SENSATION IN MY STOMACH WHEN I THINK OF YOU.
YEAH, I THINK THAT'S CALLED... BUTTERFLIES.

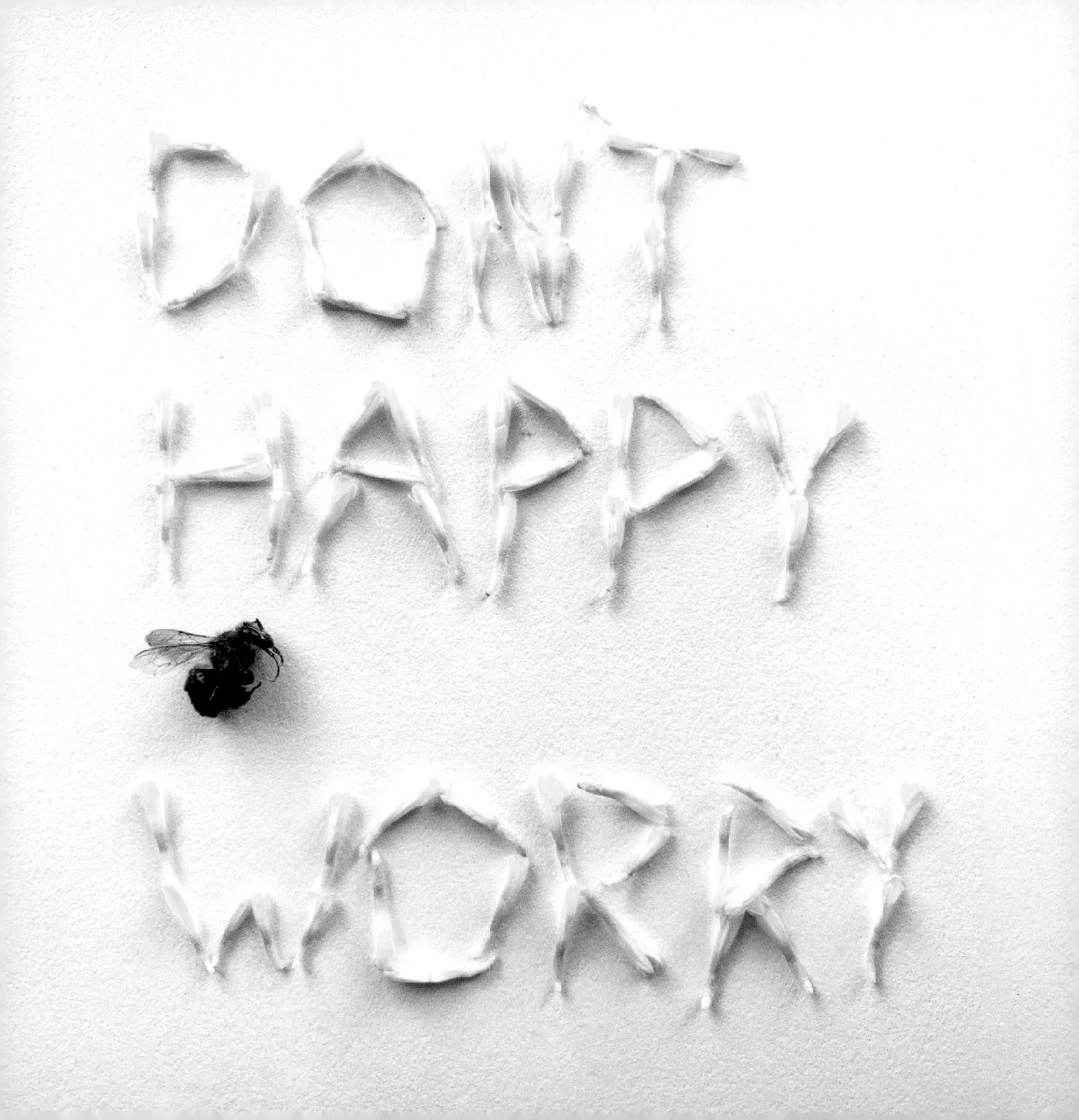
DON'T
HAPPY
WORRY

Wait, what?

until death do us part.

Awww.

THIS IS IT.

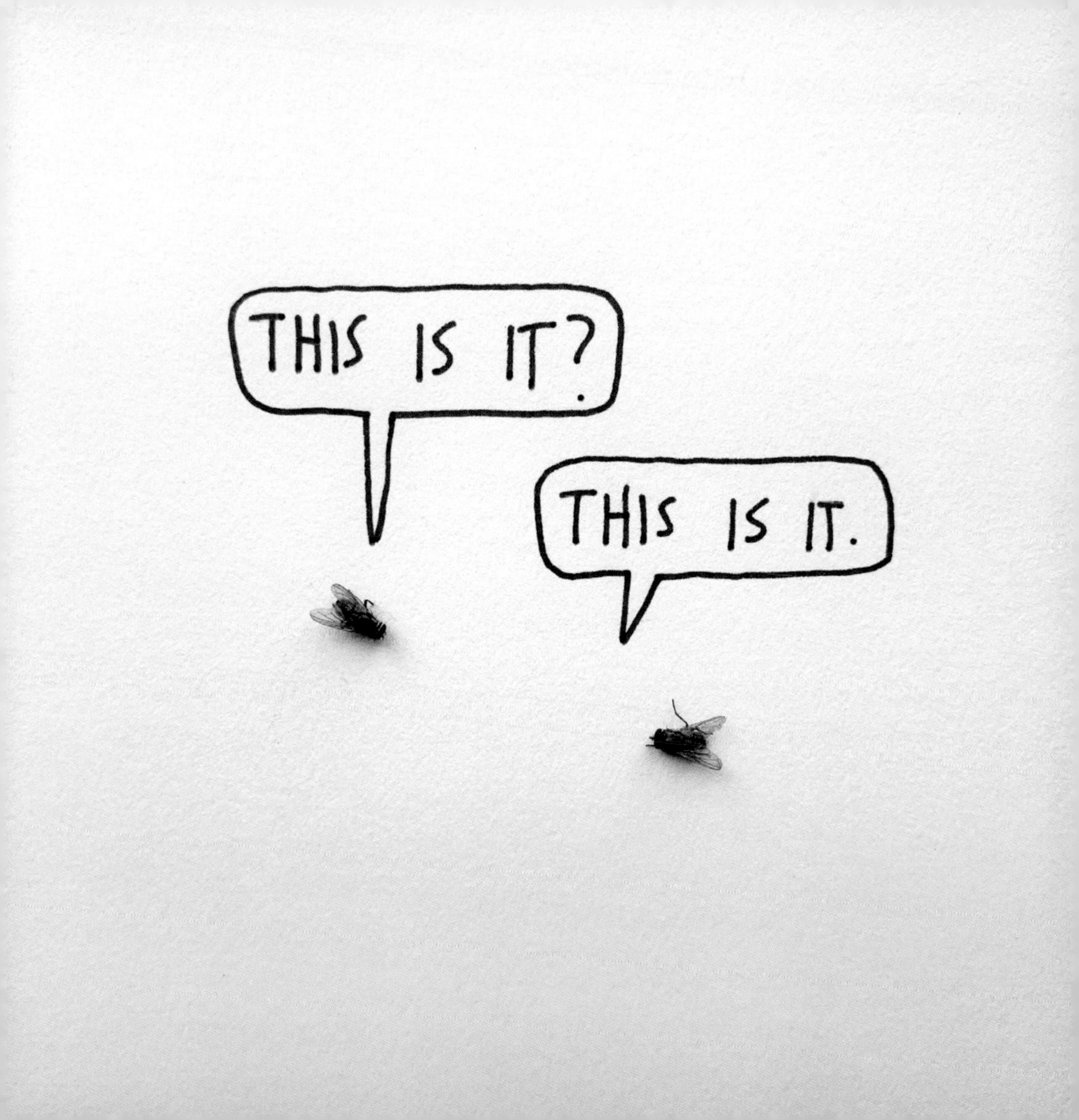
THIS IS IT?
THIS IS IT.

Nature is wild.

PANTONE
Monarch

to bee or gnat to bee?

That is the real question.

JUST BREATHE.

Inhale. Exhale. Repeat.

You give me butterflies.

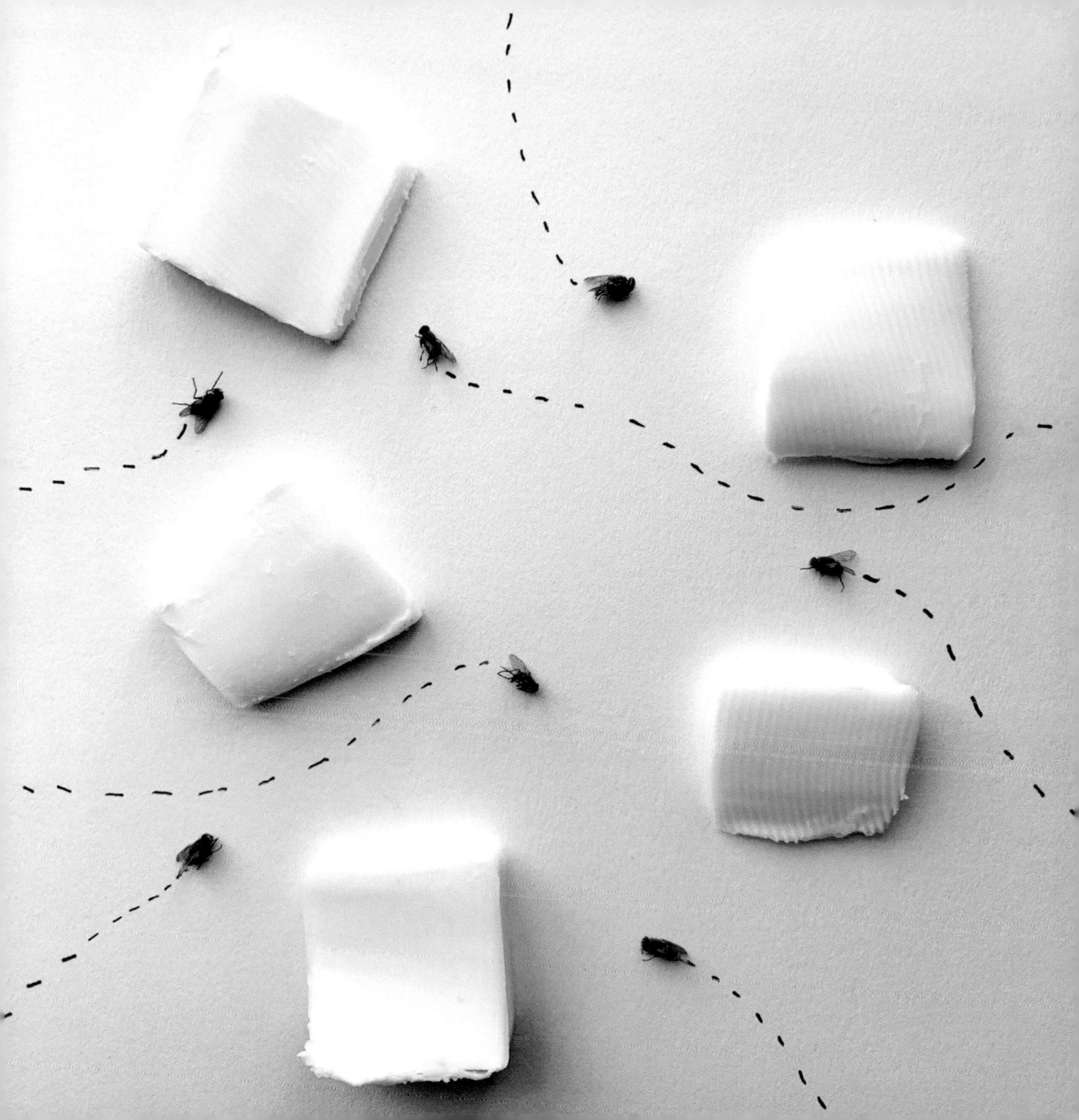

MOTH   ANDY WARHOL
                    MOTH

Moth, but make it Andy Warhol.

This is for all the single people out there.

a name given to someone you love

honey

bee vomit

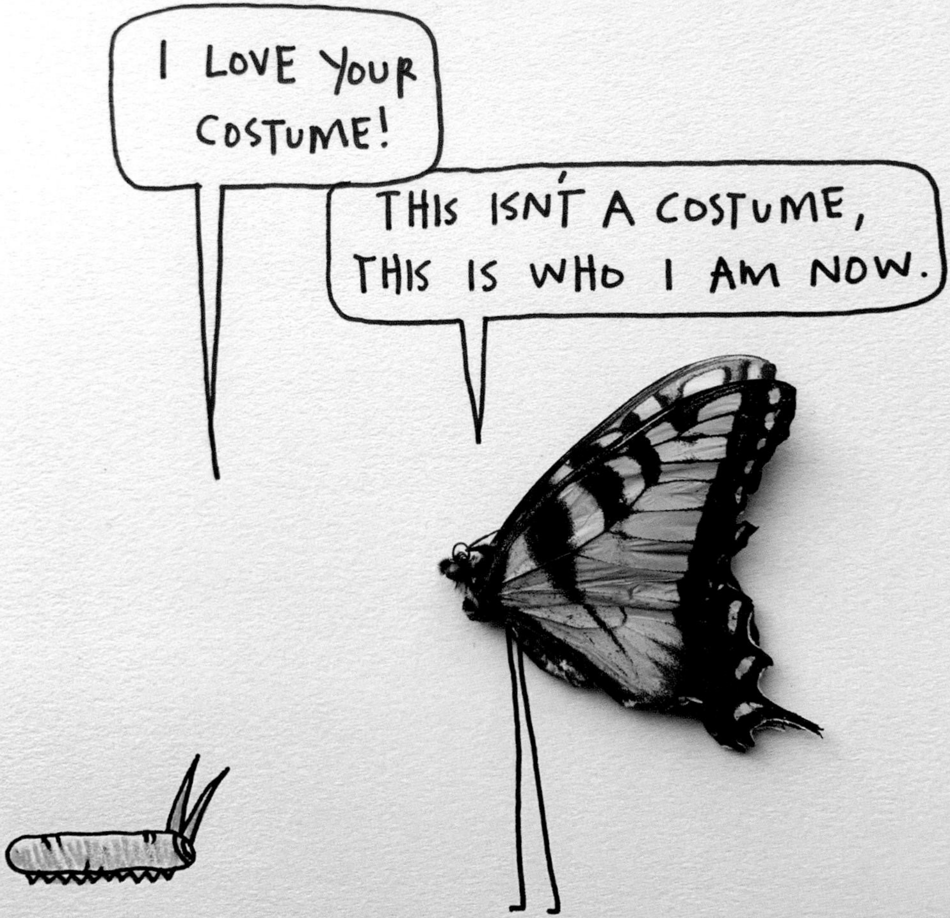
I LOVE YOUR COSTUME!
THIS ISN'T A COSTUME, THIS IS WHO I AM NOW.

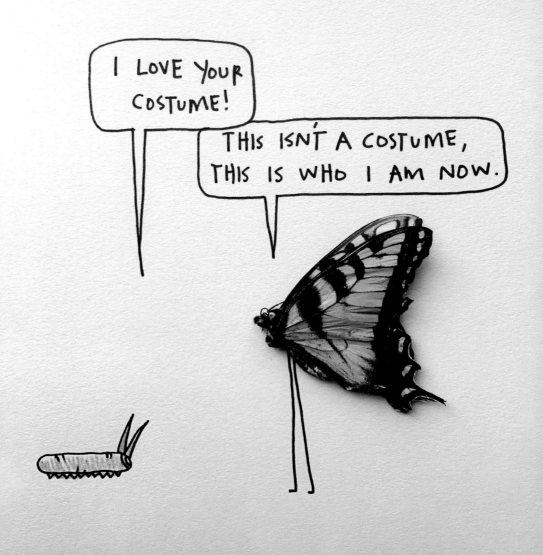

This is who I am now.

It's never too early to be thinking of your Halloween costume.

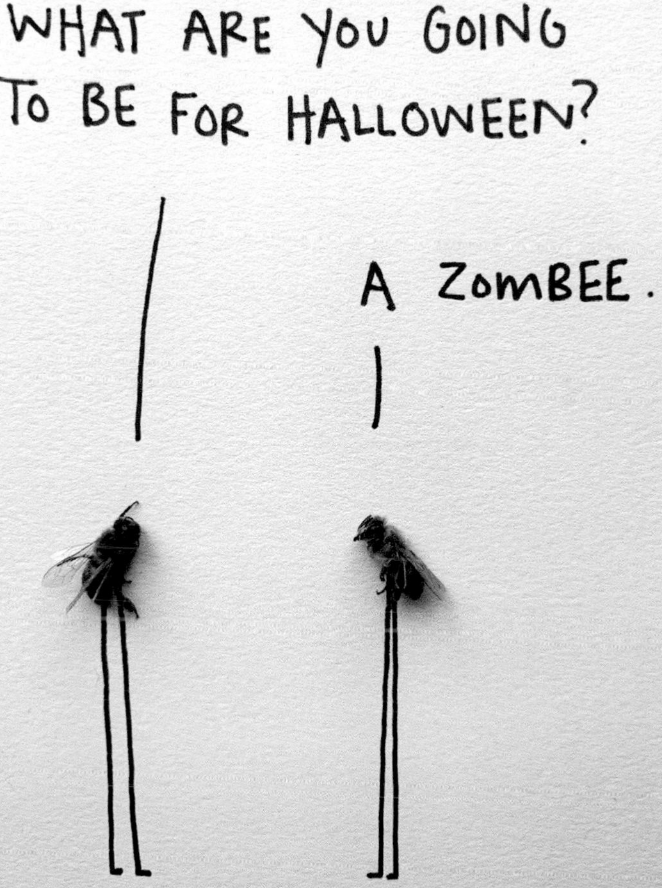
WHAT ARE YOU GOING TO BE FOR HALLOWEEN?
A ZOMBEE.

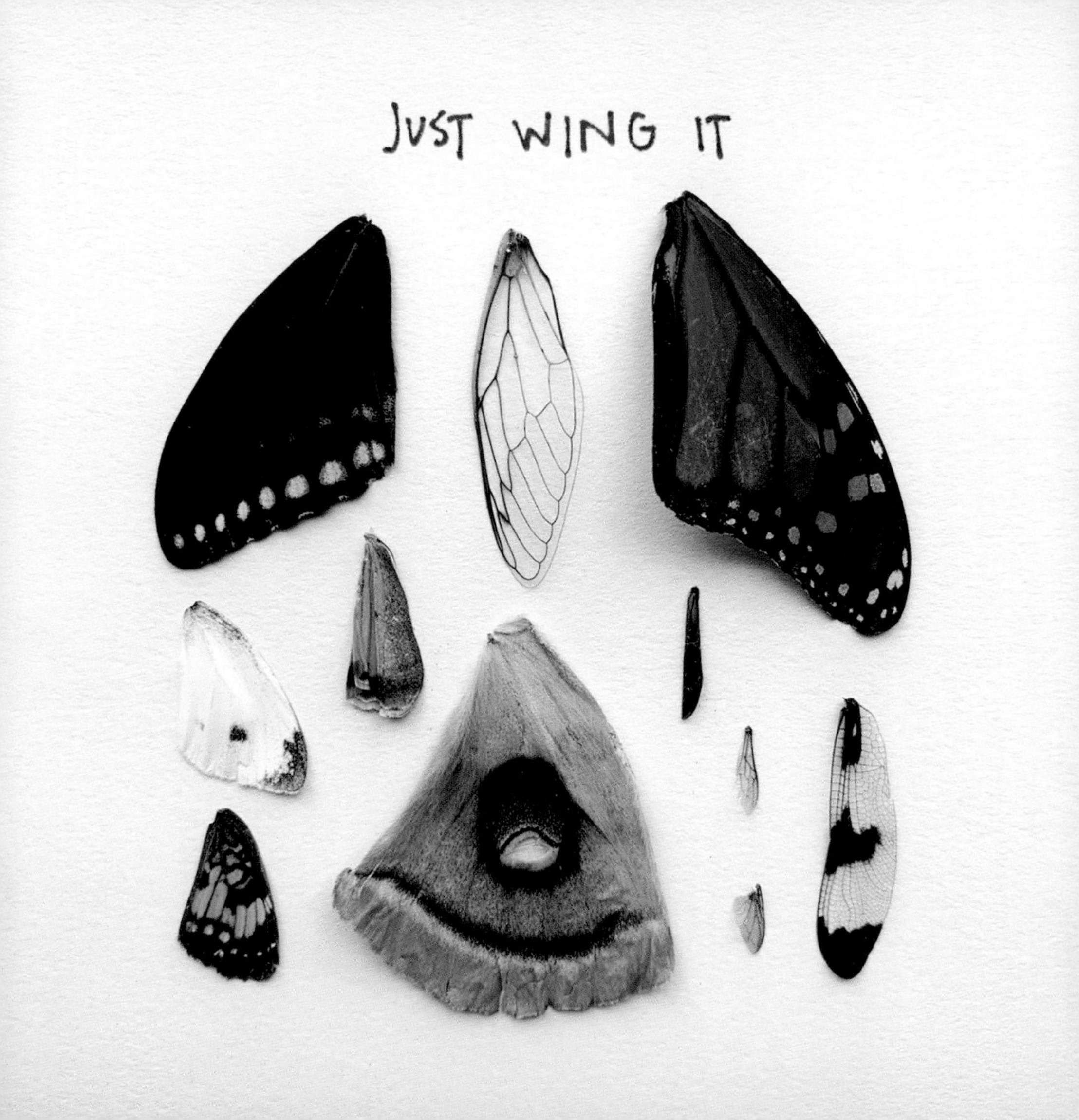
JUST WING IT

Just wing it.™

Home is where the spiderwebs are.

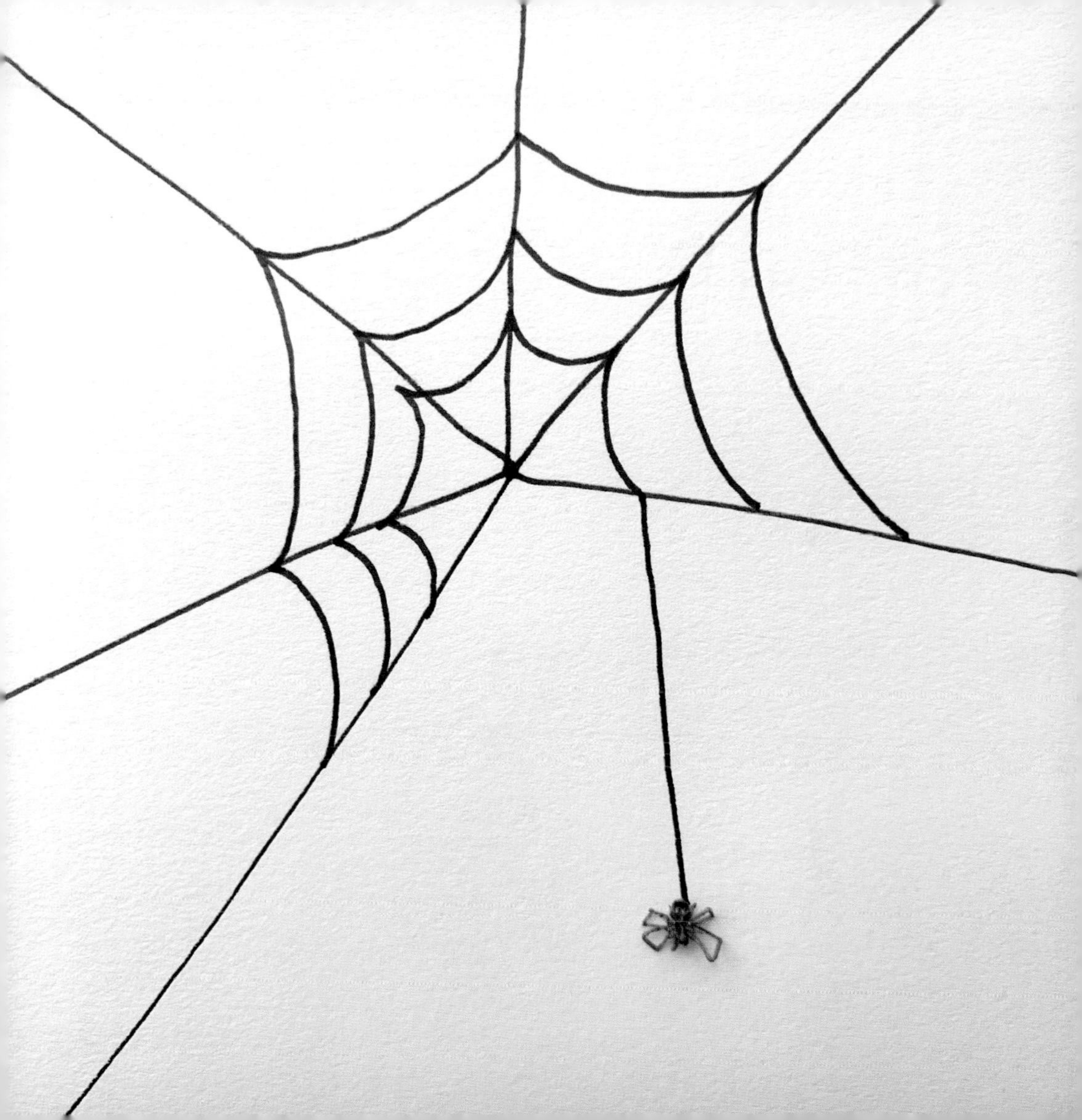

KEEP MOVING FORWARD.

Onward we go, my friends, onward.

materials needed:

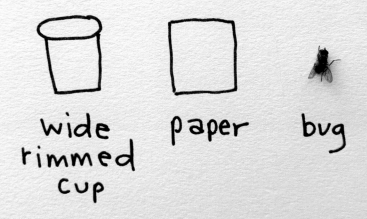

wide
rimmed
cup

paper

bug

how to catch and release
a bug :
1. get a wide rimmed cup
2. get a piece of paper
3. place cup over insect
4. slide paper under opening
5. carefully take outside
6. release

A CDEF
GHIJKLM
NOPQRST
UVWXYZ
save the bees.

Thank you for coming to my TED Talk.

ALI BECKMAN is the creator of @SoFlyTaxidermy on Instagram. In 2016, she came home one day to find two dead flies lying next to each other. She couldn't get over the image of the two flies having a conversation before they died. So, she grabbed a piece of paper, picked up the flies, got her pen out, and started drawing.

Ali lives in Bloomington, Indiana, with her dog, Georgie, and works as a hairstylist at DO Salon and as a yoga teacher at Vibe Yoga Studio. She enjoys hiking, learning about insects, and eating hot dogs at Orbit Room.

EDITORS	Ashley Runyon
	Rachel Rosolina
PROJECT MANAGER	Lesley Bolton
DESIGNER	Jennifer Witzke
COMPOSITION	Tony Brewer